THE
SCHOOLGIRL ETHIC

The
Life and Work of
Angela Brazil

Gillian Freeman

Allen Lane

Copyright © Thorpe Writers Limited, 1976

First published in 1976

Allen Lane
Penguin Books Ltd
17 Grosvenor Gardens, London SW1

ISBN 0 7139 0741 X

Printed in Great Britain by
Ebenezer Baylis and Son Ltd, The Trinity Press,
Worcester, and London

For my schoolgirl daughter
Matilda

Contents

CONTENTS

List of Illustrations

Acknowledgements

Grateful acknowledgements for assistance are due to the Arts Council of Great Britain; to Blackie & Son Limited and to the Royal United Kingdom Benefit Association for permission for the use of quotations; to Mr Anthony Davis, Director of the City of Coventry Libraries and Museums Department, for giving me access to essential material; to the Public Trustee Office; to the National Trust, the Principal Registry of the Family Division at Somerset House and to Bolton Metropolitan Arts Department for essential information.

I would especially like to thank Miss Virginia Gilbert of the Coventry Libraries Local Studies Department, Miss Helen Kranus of the Herbert Art Gallery, Mr D. J. Rimmer, Coventry City Archivist, and Mrs Valerie Wilkinson, Archivist of Coventry Cathedral.

Mr Keith Whetstone, Editor of the Coventry Evening Standard, has been an inestimable source of knowledge, support and aid throughout my research, and I would also like to thank Mr Keith Brace, Literary Editor of the Birmingham Mail, and Mr Gordon Webb, Editor of the Louth Standard, for their assistance in helping me to trace friends and acquaintances of the Brazil family.

I owe a debt of gratitude to Moray and Melvin Lloyd-Smith and to Dr Peter Bowen in Coventry and to Sheila de Burlet in Polperro for their help and hospitality; to Richard Rodney Bennett for the use of his Brazil collection; to Ruth Hall for bringing to my attention the Angela Brazil/Marie Stopes correspondence; to Alison Hawkes and Maureen Duffy for research on my behalf.

There is not space here to thank individually the past and present members of the Coventry Natural History and Scientific Society, the Coventry branch of the Y.W.C.A., the Coventry City Guild, the Cathedral committees, and the many people who have lent me photographs, written and talked to me, only some of whom are mentioned in the text, although all the contributions have been invaluable.

Finally I must pay tribute to Mrs Carol Walters, Mr A. Morris-Gilbert and Mrs E. H. Davies, whose recollections, photographs and generous expenditure of time and patience have made this book possible.

[1]
INTRODUCING
ANGELA

Angela Brazil was born in Preston, Lancashire, on St Andrew's Day, 30 November, in 1869, and she liked to claim it as part of her Celtic inheritance. Her father, Clarence Brazil, was of Irish descent, her mother, Angelica McKinnel, Scottish on the paternal side but Spanish on her mother's. Both Angelica and Angela looked Spanish, which Angela's siblings did not.

Angelica, although a British subject, was born and brought up in Rio de Janeiro (her father owned a shipping line) and it seems an odd quirk of fate that a girl from Rio should marry a man called Brazil. In those days the name was pronounced like the country, and it wasn't until after her father's death that Angela decided that the emphasis should be on the first syllable, to rhyme with *dazzle*, and dazzle she did, with her sense of cultural superiority and somewhat intimidating charm.

Mrs Brazil was thirty-four when she gave birth to Angela, her last child. There were, already, two sons, Clarence McKinnel and Walter Henry, respectively ten and eight years old, and Amy who was six. Mr Brazil was a cotton mill manager (an occupation that Angela was inclined to overlook when tracing her heritage), a man of altruistic Christian principles whose own artistic talents had been stifled by his mother, afraid that if her son went to Rome to sculpt he would be seduced by Popery.

The family had moved from Chorley to Preston sometime between the births of Amy and Angela. They lived at 1 Westcliffe Terrace, although Angela referred to the house as 'Westcliffe' in her autobiography, *My Own Schooldays*, which may have been pretension or simply the way she remembered it. In any case, the location was a well-established, middle-class one in a semi-rural position near Preston Park, and the house was large enough to accommodate not only the Brazil family of six but two living-in servants. Angela wrote of night-nursery and attics, and in the 1871 census a visitor was also accounted for, so presumably there was a spare bedroom as well. 1 Westcliffe Terrace no longer stands, having been consumed by the insatiable Victorian railway, but the Brazils moved before its decline to Egremont, a suburb on the Cheshire side of the Mersey Estuary, and again three and a half years later to Manchester.

There is no doubt that Angela's formative influence was Angelica. She was a remarkable woman, compassionate, understanding and knowledgeable. Cherished memories of freedom in her own childhood, harshly curtailed by an English boarding-school, made her determined to bring up her own children in a creative and enlightened atmosphere. Clarence (*père*), although inclined to rigorousness, allowed her a free hand with her daughters, a creditable tolerance in an age when children 'should be seen and not heard'. He called the girls his 'dear little silly billies' because they were unable to comprehend his theological phraseology, but he did not try to enforce his own brand of religious instruction. Church-going was an integral part of Angela's early routine, but it was the introduction by Angelica of art, music, literature and botany which fascinated and absorbed the four children. They were all intelligent and talented. Angela, of course, wrote and liked to act; Amy and Angela painted and sketched; Amy and Walter were musical (Angela was not but she liked to pretend she was; in fact she had little appreciation and, although she sometimes played a guitar, sang flat) and all of them were keen botanists. Clarence . . . well, apart from the botanical reference, Clarence was scissored from Angela's carefully chosen recollections for reasons which are necessarily speculative, so that it is only by a process of induction that one gathers he had a love of literature and archaeology and a lack of snobbishness the others did not share. Those who thought they knew the three younger Brazils well – and they lived together, unmarried, in Coventry from middle-age until they died – had no notion that there was an elder brother.

'They were a kind of holy trinity, weren't they?' said one gentleman who had known them for twenty-five years, and added guiltily, 'They wouldn't have liked me to say that.'

Angela was adored and admired by Amy from the day she was born, and gentle, kind, reserved Amy was dominated by Angela until her death. In appearance the sisters were dissimilar. Amy was narrow-faced, fair-haired and blue-eyed and must have resembled her father. In later years she and Walter could have been taken for twins, and in that 'holy trinity' Angela was the odd one out. She had big, compelling, dark brown eyes with large lids, and brown curly hair, and she was as rounded as the other two were angular. No photograph of Clarence has survived, and I think it is probable he had something of the McKinnel looks, although apparently he was not unlike his Brazil cousins ('the sausage makers' Angela once called them) who were eventually dropped by the holy trio even to the extent of their denying the relationship. The few stories of Clarence that Angela recalls indicate a character as strong and wilful as her own, and Angela did not like competition. She described herself (disguised as Peggy in *A Terrible Tomboy*, her first book) at the age of five, and although the account is romanticized, it must be close to the original.

The worst of it was poor Peggy did not mean to be so naughty; she was so eager, so active, so full of overflowing and impetuous life, with such restless daring and abounding energy, that in the excitement of the moment her wild spirits were apt to carry her away, simply because she never stopped to think of the consequences. She had always a hundred projects on hand, each one of which she was ready to pursue with unflagging zeal and that absorbing interest which is the secret of true enjoyment.

Such natures as Peggy's taste life to the full; for them it is never a stale or worthless draught. Each moment is so keenly lived that time flies by on eager wings, and though there may be stormy troubles sometimes, as a rule the spirit dwells like the swallows, in an upper region of joy which is scarcely dreamed of by those who cannot soar so high.

Angela had a keen appreciation of her powers of enjoyment. She had the art of suspending disbelief and would positively wallow in myth, magic and romance, and although she wrote that she never confused fact with fiction, which meant that she did not believe in fairies, there is some evidence to show that she actually did.

One of her earliest Preston memories was mortal if dramatic. She liked to use her dolls as puppets, and there was a particular story of rescue and revenge, told to her by a housemaid, which appealed to her so much that she enacted it again and again, rigging up a primitive gallows from which the heroine was snatched at the eleventh hour.

'My young blood revelled in the horror of it,' she wrote, although on a later occasion, when Clarence strung up her favourite wax doll from the curtain pole by its throat, there was no revelling.

My shrieks rent the air, and never stopped till she was cut down from her perilous position and restored to my motherly arms. I believe it took Edinburgh rock to restore harmony after this dreadful outrage.

It is interesting to note that sweets have a mollifying role in all her books.

Perhaps Clarence saw through her, or at any rate recognized the complexity of her nature. She has been described by acquaintances as intimidating, dominating and shy.

'There were at least two Angela Brazils,' one of her friends has said.

'She was three different people,' said another. Certainly there was the romantic persona she chose to project to her readers, and the calculating business woman who travelled at the expense of her publishers in order to write *The School in the South* (Italy), *Schoolgirl Kitty* (France), and *Nesta's New School* (Switzerland). There was also the ardent, genuine and generous conservationist, far ahead of her time in her awareness of the need for the preservation of land and monuments; the tireless committee woman (in Coventry she worked for the cathedral, the Y.W.C.A., and was a founder member of the City Guild); and the lady of means and manners. There was also the author of forty-nine racy schoolgirl novels packed with slang, which to most of the people who knew her was incongruously at odds with the cultured and self-consciously correct hostess who was, in the 1920s and 30s, the *doyenne* of Coventry society.

> At the head of the grand staircase
> She received me.
> Angela . . .
> Ah! She stood as a statue would
> New found in the Isles of Greece,
> Enrobed in gold and jewelled fold
> Of emerald green and bright cerise.*

Thus wrote Abe Jephcott, a local poet, in a long poem entitled 'Connoisseurs' in which he described his visit to the Brazil residence and pronounced Angela 'Queen of Literature' – an

* See Appendix B.

epithet hardly suited to the creator of drawling Daisy Davenport, 'Queen of the Dormitory', and of forthright Olivia Penrose, title-heroine of 'The Queer Girl at St Quentin's', a short story published in the *Girls' Own Paper* in March 1940, only five months after Abe Jephcott's paean of praise in the *Coventry Standard*.

Angela's own schooldays began in Preston at the Miss Knowles's Select Ladies' School, where she spent one disastrous morning. Angelica must have decided that the nursery at Westcliffe Terrace was too narrow a confinement for her lively four-year-old daughter, and since kindergarten was a concept unknown except to the most advanced educationalists, an arrangement was made for Angela to accompany Amy to the refined establishment she attended. Angela, brought up in an environment in which she had been encouraged to express herself freely, did not understand the seriousness of 'self-discipline', and when the younger Miss Knowles took the new pupil on her knee to explain the necessity of decorous behaviour, Angela put her arms round Miss Eleanor's neck and, staring earnestly into her eyes, removed the lady's hairpins until the coils of her hair fell most undecorously onto her shoulders.

'She banished me from the comfort of her knee to the cold desert of a hard form,' Angela recalled, 'and told a girl named Beatrice to teach me to knit.'

Perhaps Angela's understanding of the schoolgirl spirit began that morning. Creative learning, the channelling of enthusiasms which she had experienced at home, was to appear again and again in her books, fulfilling the needs of her fictional heroines in a way which her own schools failed to do. She understood youthful exuberance, both mental and physical, and was a great champion of hockey, not only for the controlled release of adolescent energy, but as the bridge between staffroom and classroom. In 1924, looking back at her own unsporting schooldays, she wrote:

> The introduction of games is no doubt largely responsible for the removal of the old-fashioned barrier which used to exist between governess and pupil. We should no more have dreamt of our dignified headmistress indulging in hockey than (forgive the simile!) we should have expected to see St Peter, halo, keys and all, engaged in a tussle at football. It was simply unthinkable.

In Coventry she was a familiar figure on the sidelines, watching the games between rival local schools, even involving herself by setting a prize essay for the best account of a match. 'To be able to write for young people', she said in *Answers* in 1923, depends, I consider, largely upon whether you are able to retain your early attitude of mind while acquiring a certain facility with your pen. It is a mistake ever to grow up! I confess I am still an absolute schoolgirl in my sympathies.

This was borne out, not only in her novels, but in her life. An inveterate party-giver, Angela gave children's parties even to her adult guests. Alcohol was seldom served, but there were cakes and jellies, charades and games with prizes. When she concluded *A Terrible Tomboy* with a description of the now mature Peggy, the element of self-praise is unmistakable.

> Peggy does not feel the least bit older than when she climbed the water-wheel, or thrashed Jones Minor behind the paling of the cricket-field – if growing older means losing your ideals, and your keen enthusiasm, and your hopefulness, and a certain appreciation of other people's worth which is our birthright when we are young. She is still capable of climbing a tree or scrambling over a hedge when no-one is looking, and pursuing her hobbies with all her former vigour and energy. She is sometimes almost ashamed of feeling, as she says, so ridiculously young, but after all one's age should not be measured by one's years, and wherever she may go, or whatever she may do, Peggy will keep that most priceless of possessions, the heart of a little child, without which, equally in this world or the next, it is impossible to enter into the kingdom of heaven.

Angela did not begin to write seriously until she was in her thirties, and she was thirty-six when *A Terrible Tomboy* was published with illustrations by Amy and herself. It was inevitable that this, being her first full-length book, should have some of the religious undertones and Victorian overtones associated with her own earliest reading. She said of Peggy/Angela:

> Do I make too much of the little girl, who, after all, was no heroine, but who tried her honest best, like many another, to fear God, tell the truth, and love her neighbour as herself? If so, my love for her bright ways and warm heart must be my excuse, for I have told Peggy's story just as it happened.

A Terrible Tomboy was not a school story; those came later, almost by chance, following the success of *The Fortunes of Philippa*, which was based on Angelica's experiences of English school life (and behaviour and climate) after her first decade in the warmth of Rio de Janeiro. The style which was to establish itself as vintage Brazil with *A Fourth Form Friendship* in 1911 had scarcely begun to emerge. Surprisingly, in a form as defined and repetitive as a 'school story', there are continuous conscious and subconscious references to the events and emotional conflicts of Angela's own life: a gallery of sympathetic and deeply loved mothers, frequently known as 'Muvvie' to their daughters; fathers who play only distant roles; headmistresses who reflect Angela's width of interests and are, in their way, surrogate mothers; and of course there are the friendships between the girls (and sometimes between teachers and girls) with passions, jealousies and misunderstandings, demands of loyalty and honesty, and kisses and embraces which today would be interpreted both sexually and psychologically.

'D'you know,' said Meg Chadwick, sitting on Muriel Cameron's bed, with one arm round the waist of Loie Donaldson and another clasped round the neck of Natalie Robyns. 'D'you know, I can't think what's come over Daisy Davenport lately. She's quite changed, isn't she?'
'Rather!' agreed Loie emphatically. 'She's not the same girl. I used to be chums with Daisy last term; but now – it's altogether off!'*

Physical contact, keeping pace with the sophistication of the times, progressed from sleeping enrapt with the chosen friend ('Would you care to come and creep in with me? I've got a hot bottle')† to total bodily disassociation in Angela's final books. By the late 1930s she was in any case writing to a formula, and her style (which makes the work between 1910 and 1931 a collector's joy) had deteriorated and become perfunctory, although she was no less popular among girls, or unpopular with headmistresses, who saw 'the works', as Angela herself referred to them, as threats to their authority.

On the first day of the autumn term in 1936, a new girl to St Paul's in London was stunned by a dramatic address from Ethel Strudwick, the principal, who at morning prayers expressed the wish to collect the books of Angela Brazil and burn them. It is all

* *Queen of the Dormitory.*
† *Margaret's Room Mate* (*British Girls' Annual*, 1912), subtitled *The Entente Cordiale in School Life.*

the more astonishing when one considers the amount of sheer knowledge that Angela inculcated into her stories, widening the horizons of her readers in so many spheres, literary, geographical, historical, archaeological and botanical, as well as creating awareness of music and the visual arts. Her vocabulary, too, was extensive; there was no paucity of words, no repetition as was prevalent in, say, Enid Blyton, who in 1936 was rapidly ascending to prime popularity. Was it the slang that upset Miss Strudwick? Even that was dated, and I wonder if it was ever spoken, although a number of women who were schoolgirls in Coventry assure me that Angela used them for copy. Did girls really ask one another, 'Twiggez vous?' or acquiesce with, 'Right you are, O Queen! It's a blossomy idea!'? Did they, even in 1917, murmur, 'Strafe the old chap and his jaw-wag,' and if they did, was it harmful? Perhaps it was a forthrightness about examinations as a method for acquiring knowledge that made Miss Strudwick anxious for the future of her girls, fearing that, with Ermie Hall of Kingfield High, in *Loyal to the School*, they might scorn the system.

'Miss Pratt says airily: "Do an extra hour of prep", but I find the longer I work the stupider I am. VA isn't going to get much credit out of *me* in the exams. I always forget things when I see the questions and remember them afterwards when it's too late and they're no use.'

'Don't say "no use",' preached Carrie.

'Yes, I *do* say "no use", Carrie Turner, so don't be sanctimonious. Geometry and Latin may be all right in an exam room, but what good are they going to be to me when I'm middle-aged and married?'

'Perhaps you'll never be either.'

'Oh come! Don't consign me to an early grave or perpetual spinsterhood. *I* think exams are a relic of the barbarous ages, and they ought to be banished, with thumb screws, and the rack, and all other instruments of torture. I'd like to write to the newspapers about it.'

The grousing of certain unwilling victims in VA made no difference at all to the examinations, which approached as relentlessly as the car of a juggernaut, and as unfailingly as the seasons. A few favoured brains in the form enjoyed them, but the majority, including Lesbia, heaved sighs of relieved anticipation when the inky ordeal was over.

None of this was to say that Angela Brazil did not believe in hard work. Her own education at Ellerslie, in Manchester, was exceptionally thorough, and the staff excelled in the teaching of English literature. Whatever was lacking in the way of organized games or the stimulating pursuit of extra-curricular activities, the academic standard was demanding. Angela, who could have gone on to university with others from her class, decided that she would rather study art. 'I was not built on academic lines,' she said. 'It was the romantic and imaginative side of a subject that always gripped me.' The 'year's hard grind' for the Higher Cambridge Certificate killed any desire for college life.

'Do you remember the Cambridge days,' an old schoolfriend wrote to her, 'when you used to go on reciting page after page of Morley, the rest of us putting in a scrappy half page now and then?'

Ellerslie girls were expected to learn by heart sixty pages of Morley's *English Literature* in preparation for each lesson, to have the biography and works of 'every author since the Saxon heptarchy at our fingers' ends'. This was the basis, combined with an extensive knowledge of botany derived from her mother and a natural disposition towards archaeology and history, from which Angela continued to study, learn and appreciate for the rest of her life, facilities she passed on to generations of girls.

'If you are writing a biography of her I shall be delighted,' one of her 1920s fans wrote to me. 'It is fashionable today to laugh at her type of story, but I am extremely grateful to her for all I learned from her when, after rheumatic fever, I spent endless hours reading her books.' Angela wrote:

I have always had the strong feeling that if I had added B.A. to my name, forced myself into a scholastic mould, and become a headmistress, I should never, never, *never* have written stories about schoolgirls, at any rate not from the schoolgirl's point of view, which is the attitude that has appealed to me most.

Whatever interpretation one might put upon Angela Brazil's Peter Pan complex – and several theories spring to the contemporary mind – she herself was innocent of them. Writing for pleasure (and for money) she conceived a sense of duty to impart a code of honourable behaviour to British girls, while acknowledging that this often meant an inner struggle with the baser self. The zest and enjoyment with which she communicated her interests and beliefs ensured her a readership for almost three quarters of a century and a sale of three million books under the Blackie imprint alone (her most popular title, *The Nicest Girl in the School*, sold 153,000 copies). At the peak of her fame her income would have boggled the mind of the man who called her 'a dear little silly billy', her father, the late Clarence Brazil.

[2]
MAROONED!

The English are particularly prone to romanticize their school-days. Why else should elderly men sport their old school ties and link themselves to hundreds of disparate males solely because they were taught in the same classrooms and ate inferior meals in the same dining-halls, not necessarily even in the same decade?

Angela Brazil was young enough and old enough to benefit from the changes that were affecting women's education.

> To us there was no school like Ellerslie, and, after leaving, the mere fact of meeting a former pupil was sufficient to make an instant bond.

Miss Millington, her headmistress, was an enlightened educationalist with many of the qualities that immortalized Miss Buss, the famous founder of the North London Collegiate and Camden Schools. Queen's College in London, the first day-school to attempt the new style of education, had been open for twenty years when Angela was born, so that by the time she was ten and ready for serious teaching, most major cities had at least one good school for girls. They were patronized by the increasing and aspiring middle classes, who, unable to afford private governesses, were also not prepared to sacrifice their daughters to the national schools for the poor. The aristocracy continued to educate its girls at home, but affluent Victorian tradesmen believed that ladies were not only born but could be made if parents paid the price. The majority of Angela Brazil's 'girls' came from homes materially less endowed than her own had been – but their fathers were never 'in trade'.

Cheltenham Ladies' College, which took both boarders and day pupils, was, under the renowned Miss Beale, the pattern for

23

pioneering principals. Miss Anderson, who founded Ellerslie in Victoria Park, Manchester (it closed in the 1920s when the neighbourhood became unfashionable), was in all probability a member of the newly formed northern Schoolmistresses' Association and the North of England Council for Higher Education of Women. Both had been instigated by Anne Clough, sister of the poet, Arthur. Anne Clough's own little school at Ambleside in Westmorland was, in the 1850s, progressive in its all-round teaching (Greek history and starching) but almost as harsh as Lowood when it came to physical comforts. There were only two boarders, Mary Arnold (granddaughter of Doctor Arnold of Rugby), who later became the writer Mrs Humphrey Ward, and Sophie Bellasis, whose memories were published in the Cornhill Magazine by her husband T. C. Down in June 1920.

> There was no coddling or self-indulgence of any sort whatever; she never indulged herself and did not allow it of anybody in her house. There was no lying in bed, nor hot water in the mornings, we had to wash the winter through with lumps of ice in the basin.

Miss Anderson, advanced in matters of education, was also old-fashioned in other respects, and even Miss Millington, who succeeded her the term that Angela Brazil joined the school, did not allow the girls sufficient freedom, although she did permit the reading of fiction, previously forbidden. What Angela wanted was societies, school plays, a lending library, and, of course, games.

> Beyond a weekly class for calisthenics and drill we had no exercise whatever. That was considered a matter for our home people to attend to after 4.30. There was no provision for cricket, hockey or tennis.

Soon after she left, hockey *was* introduced as part of the curriculum. Miss Beale had set the precedent (as in so many ways) at Cheltenham. Her first reaction on seeing the game played was (so the story goes) to exclaim in horror, 'The children will hurt themselves if they all run after one ball. Get some more balls at once!' Then, with typical adjustment to a new idea, she promptly made arrangements to finance the best possible pitch. (Lacrosse came later, when Louisa Lumsden, headmistress of St Andrew's – now St Leonard's – saw it played by North American Indians and pronounced it perfect for her girls.)

How Angela envied this new generation!

When I go to see modern girls' schools, and know what jolly times they have with games and clubs and acting, I feel I missed a very great deal ... Quite shortly after I left Ellerslie, the headmistress, always keenly alive to modern influences, completely reorganised matters ... I felt aggrieved beyond words ... Perhaps the influence of the malevolent planet Saturn in my horoscope retarded matters, and released the jolly times at Ellerslie only when I was off the horizon!

She was an unflagging seeker of 'jolly times', and resented her schools for failing to provide them. As an adult she organized picnics and parties and musical evenings (which were sometimes jollier for her than for her guests), but as a child fun was necessarily ex-curricular. While the schools she created compensated for Ellerslie's recreational deficiencies, the 'adventures' that beset her many heroines had their basis in reality. Angela, to the end of her life, transfigured minor incidents into Significant Experiences, and one of the first was Being Marooned, a predicament her readers might safely anticipate whenever there was a coastal setting.

'We're marooned! That's what it amounts to,' uttered Deirdre to Dulcie in a shaking voice in *The School by the Sea*.

'We're marooned, that's what it is,' stammered Aveline to Raymonde in *The Madcap of the School*.

'I've had an awful time, lost in the cave and marooned here for hours,' exclaimed Brenda, half-laughing and half-crying, in *The School on the Moor*.

'It sounds so thrilling when you read it,' said Myfanwy in *A Fourth Form Friendship*, 'but when you're cold and hungry it takes the romance away.'

'You're a guide, aren't you?' said practical Rosemunde to helpless Anne, marooned in *The School on the Cliff*. 'Do you know some morse?'

Disobedience, foolishness and natures too intrepid for their own good brought terrifying moments to the girls and unnecessary anguish to friends, parents and teachers.

'Girls! Girls! Where have you been?' cried Miss Drummond of Birkwood, 'with such a look on her pale face that they realized for the first time what she must have suffered all the hours of that anxious night.'

'You provided a nice birthday treat for Miss Birks, I must

say,' commented Jessie Macpherson sarcastically to Dulcie and Deidre, while Miss Birks herself 'said little, but they knew it was the ominous silence before the storm.'

'What did she say?' whispered Ardiune, Morvyth and Katherine, as they escorted Avelyne and Raymonde from Miss Beasley's study. 'All recreation stopped for three days, and learn the whole of Gray's Elegy!' choked the sinners.

'Gray's Elegy! You'll never do it! Oh, you poor chickens! The Bumble can be a perfect beast sometimes! I say, what was it like on the island?' 'Top-hole!' responded Raymonde as she mopped her eyes.

The island on which Angela found herself marooned was merely an area of sand left by the neap-tide at Sunderland Point, but she thought the whole episode 'top-hole'. She was only four, the family still lived at Preston but spent their holidays at Morecambe Bay. In the 1870s Sunderland was rural and remote, primroses grew along the sandy lanes, and Angela, who was able to name wild flowers with accuracy at an age when most children recognize only buttercups and daisies, recollected 'yellow horned poppy on the shore and viper's bugloss, and lungwort and houndstongue', no doubt making her discoveries alongside Angelica who was busy recording rare finds in her copy of John's *Flowers of the Field*. It was here, too, that Angela made her first collection of stones, shells and seaweed (a fact of which I was reminded as I looked through boxes labelled *Brazil Collection* in the basement of Coventry's Herbert Art Gallery and Museum, and came across long dead and dusty starfish, and paper sheets stuck with crumbling kelp).

The Brazils stayed at Sunderland Hall, which was on an extreme promontory, and 'went everywhere, even to church', by boat. Grandmother Brazil accompanied them, and in the manner of the times behaved like an old lady although she was only in her middle sixties. In winter she sat knitting by the fire, with a French silk shawl round her shoulders. In summer, by the sea, she sat in a bath-chair drawn by a donkey, with Angela riding on the step, and once the conveyance overturned and flung Angela into the hedge. This escapade dimmed in importance to the thrill of being cut off by the tide (or *almost* cut off by the tide) with Walter and Amy and two local boys, Tom and Dickie Townley, who were their escorts.

To Angela, the sand island was a treasure island, a repository for flotsam. She found a toy boat, a walking-stick and a dead porpoise, which appealed to her most. The prolonged study of this interesting corpse took the children's attention from the incoming sea, and it was only frantic shouts from the mainland which drew attention to their plight. While Walter escorted Amy, waist-high, through the waves, the two gallant Townley boys carried Angela between them. 'I liked the boys as sea-horses,' she said, 'and would gladly have careered farther over the ocean, a juvenile Amphitrite in Neptune's Kingdom.'

It was a typical response. 'Neptune's Kingdom' cast a spell on Angela, or rather, she wove it for herself, a deliberate state of self-entrancement. She liked to dwell on the sea's power over the life and death of mortals, a theme which recurred constantly in her work. The autobiographical Peggy is the first to voice it in *A Terrible Tomboy*.

'I've always thought I should like to be a foundling,' said Peggy. 'It is so delightfully mysterious to be picked up from a wreck on the sea shore . . . and nobody knows who you are, or anything about you. They always keep your beautiful baby-clothes, and the gold locket round your neck with the portrait inside, and then, when you're grown up, you turn out to be the only daughter of a duke, who has been mourning for you ever since you were lost.'

It wasn't a gold locket which proved the identity of Johnnie Turner in *Ruth of St Ronan's*, but Ruth Hilton's amulet, given to her by her *ayah* as she departed from India for an English education. Before the wreck of the *Mauria*, Ruth gave one part to her chum, Johnnie, who, like herself, was saved from the sea. A chance meeting restored both friendship and amulet, and Johnnie to his rightful parents. His father wasn't a duke, or even titled, but a closer version of Peggy's daydream was the story of little Wavie, the golden-haired infant of *A Gift from the Sea*, a story first published in *The Chummy Book*, a Nelson anthology, and later on its own. Joan Bramley, who, like her creator, indulged in fantasies of orphans from the deep, importuned Neptune with a note in a bottle. A convenient torpedo (the story was written in 1918) washed up Wavie, so named by the impoverished Bramleys because the waves had borne her to them. Back in London, Joan began to be preyed upon by guilt. Wavie might have a real family somewhere, pining for her. A chance meeting in Hyde Park with Sir Denis and Lady Vernon of Horton Towers, Dorset, revealed

Wavie to be their beloved only grandchild, Violet, orphaned when her mother died at sea. Their son Bernard, married to a 'charming American lady', had joined his regiment 'to fight for Britain's honour', never to return. His widow and baby daughter were on their way to Horton Towers when the torpedo struck. Reward for the Bramleys was a house on the Dorset estate, allowing Joan to remain close to Wavie for the remainder of her childhood.

It was another young widow with a baby (a son on this occasion) who, without revealing her name to the landlord or the nurse who attended her, died in *A Fortunate Term*. Bevis was brought up by simple country folk, but breeding will out, and it took Mavis and Merle (two of Angela's most popular heroines) to establish him as Lord of the Manor.

'Uncle David,' asked Mavis, 'if those papers are proved does it mean that The Warren and the whole of Chagmouth will belong to Bevis? Is he the grandson of General Talland?'

'So Chagmouth belongs to Bevis,' repeated Merle wonderingly. 'The house, the grounds, and the woods and the shooting, and the farms, and the town are Bevis's. It's like a fairy tale!'

Isobel Stewart in *Bosom Friends* declared:

'It's just like a fairy tale. I never thought when I sat on top of the Scar that afternoon, looking down at the lovely house and garden and saying what I would do if I lived there, that it could ever really come to pass.'

Restored to *her* grandfather, Colonel Stewart, 'she filled the vacant place of the little daughter he had lost in former years,' while her mother, widowed by the Boer War, was received into the family that had previously refused to accept her. Like so many of Angela's plots, it turned on forgiveness.

Bosom Friends was her third book, following the successful *Fortunes of Philippa* (which also had a shipwreck in its final chapter), though it was published by Nelson's. From then on she was constant to Blackie's with her novels. In 1909 she was still drawing very directly on her own experiences. Silversands, the resort in which Isobel Stewart wins her grandfather's heart, was Sunderland Point, amalgamated with close-by Arneside, where the Brazil family spent later holidays. Angela described it in detail, the narrow streets cut into the cliff face, the fishing nets drying over railings and walls, the flat skates and conger eels nailed above the cottage doorways for curing. Everything had remained in her

memory, from the smell of the fish market on the quay to the
fishermen's concern with tides and storms, and the modern portion
of Arneside standing apart from the main town, the harbinger of
the seaside resort, 'yet guiltless of pier, promenade, band or
niggers', but with a parade of shops displaying buckets and spades
and shell-purses and photographic views. Her pursuits were as
carefully recorded. Her seaweed collection became Isobel's, whose
mother explained the method of mounting which Angela used for
the examples now in the Herbert Museum.

'First I'm going to fill this basin with clean water, and put
this pretty pink piece to float on it. Now, you see, I am slipping
this sheet of notepaper underneath, and drawing it very carefully
and gently from the water, so that the seaweed remains spread
out on the paper. I shall pin the sheet by its four corners on to
this board, and when it is dry you'll find that the seaweed had
stuck to the paper as if it had been glued.'

The shells were mentioned in the same chapter ('she had many
rare and beautiful kinds, from pearly cowries to scallops and
wentletraps') and Isobel recorded, fortunately by number and not
by name, forty varieties of wild flowers.

A visit that the whole family made to Arneside tower 'was
stamped on my romantic mind', said Angela. She resuscitated it
first as Silversands Tower, and then elsewhere in the 'works'; it
was instantly recognizable by the thick-stemmed ivy and 'loophole
windows', a term of which she was fond.

Here it is as Silversands Tower:

Situated at the foot of a tall wooded hill called The Scar, its
battered walls faced the long valley to the north, up which in
olden days a strict watch must have been kept for border
raiders. The ancient turreted keep, with its tiny loophole
windows, was still standing, half covered with ivy, the hairy
stems of which were as thick as small trees, and a narrow winding staircase led on to the battlements, from whence you might
see, on the one hand, the green slopes of the woods, and on the
other the yellow cliffs which bounded the blue waters of the bay.

Here it is as Marlowe Grange in *The Madcap of the School*:

Perhaps the most ancient part was the fortified gateway,
ruinous and covered with ivy, but still preserving its winding
stair leading to an upper storey that spanned the entrance. With

its tiny loophole windows and its great solid oak gate with the little door cut through it, it had the aspect of a medieval fortress.

Here it is in Angela's last book, *The School on the Loch*, having survived sixty-five years in her mental files.

It was a picturesque ruin. The crumbled walls were covered with ivy, where jackdaws were flitting about and cawing, and the ground was a grass-plot where a mass of little daisies were blooming and turning golden centres and white-fringed petals to the sun.

It was virtually the same scene that she had written forty years before in *Bosom Friends*:

The courtyard was covered with short green grass spangled with daisies, where a pair of tame ravens were solemnly hopping about, while the ivy was the home of innumerable jackdaws that flapped away at the approach of strangers, uttering their funny spoilt 'caw' as if indignant at having their haunts disturbed.

Another memorable visit Angela made during one of her early holidays was to a ruined abbey. She recalls it in her autobiography:

As if it were yesterday I can recall an expedition to Cocker-sand Abbey, where the crumbling remains of an old monastery rose grey among the surrounding rocks. As usual we went by boat, and part of the interest of the excursion was the balk which long ago the monks had fashioned to catch their fish.

The episode turns up, almost word for word, in *Bosom Friends*, with the 'crumbling remains' and the balk, and a little Irish terrier which had impressed the infant Angela.

I remember the retreating water running through the meshes, leaving the leaping shining fish stranded on the sand, and a clever little dog that ran about catching the flukes and carrying them back to his master like a retriever.

Isobel, like Angela, watched the dog with excited interest. The baby of the Brazils must have been an intensely observant child.

The transposition of her life into her art is a recognizable sub-structure to all the books, although it has a declining liveliness, at its freshest in *Bosom Friends*, its most revealingly Freudian in *For the School Colours* and *A Patriotic Schoolgirl*, and at its dullest in everything she wrote after 1935 when her own 'golden term' of creativity was replaced by Mr Blackie's yearly need for a golden manuscript.

[3]
FRIENDS AND A FIRE

Angela's shell collection, begun at Sunderland Point, continued at Egremont. When the Brazils moved from Preston, Angela was able to enjoy the freedom she had previously known only on holiday. A town child, confined to Preston Park, she revelled in the long rambling walks she was now able to take with her brothers and sisters, establishing a habit she kept all her life. Walter, who gave her pick-a-backs home from New Brighton and Leasoe in Cheshire when she was five, drove her home at fifty-five from Kenilworth and Corley, when she tramped out in her tweeds and galoshes with the Coventry Natural History and Scientific Society, of which she was an active member.

When the Brazils arrived in Egremont it was still comparatively small, and Angela remembered

> wide stretches of bright gleaming sand, where the spring tide had strewn beautiful shells, attractive rock pools like miniature aquariums, sandhills that seemed as vast and eternal as the desert, a fairytale wood where bluebells grew, a moor with blackberries and a flaming sunset, and a mysterious 'Rhododendron Gardens' where we occasionally found the world a mass of pink blossom.

Even more romantic were the ships that steamed and sailed into Mersey Harbour, feeding her twin fantasies of travel and survival. Ruth (of St Ronan's), rescued from the wreck of the *Mauria* by the steamship *Alexandra*, disembarked at Liverpool. So did impetuous American Gipsy Latimer who became *The Leader of the Lower School*, when she was picked up from a lifeboat from the ill-fated *Queen of the Waves*.

'Thank God we're saved!' exclaimed Mr Latimer.

'She's only fainted from exhaustion,' she could hear the doctor saying. 'We'll soon have her right again. Ah, here comes the beef tea!'

It was to Liverpool that Gipsy returned when she ran away from Briarcroft in the hope of working her passage to South Africa, and it was from Liverpool that Lesbia Ferrars ran back to Kingfield School instead of sailing on the *Roumania* to a new life in Canada. Lesbia's impressions were based on Angela's own when she was conducted by the captain over an emigrant ship bound for Canada. She suffered her first fears of darkness and claustrophobia as she was led along the narrow companionways (not helped by Clarence who had suggested that a bear might have sneaked aboard and be waiting in one of the tiny cabins for a chance to gobble her up), and Lesbia's horror of the cramped quarters, stuffiness and oily smell reflected them. ('She could not – no she *could* not be boxed up with those children all the way across the Atlantic!')

Did Angela, crossing on the ferry steamer, imagine herself sailing away to distant shores as she passed the foreign vessels lying in the harbour? Grandfather McKinnel had owned the first steamship line to ply between Liverpool and Rio, and the family still had relations living there. Tales of a cousin who had died of the dreaded yellow fever, together with the occasional sight of the Yellow Jack ('that fatal flag' Angela called it) gave her another kind of thrill. She yearned for adventure and danger and the hint of mystery. Chinese and Indian sailors, exotic cargoes and the omnipresent threat of drowning worked on her youthful imagination. She was, in the years to come, an indefatigable traveller.

For the time being, however, apart from the annual holiday at Morecambe Bay, life was suburban but the mind fertile. A garden was never just a garden to Angela, it was a fairy haunt; her toys were all alive. Her hoop, Tommy, she said, liked to go for walks; balls had individual characteristics and names; there was Tatianathy (a plaid one), Iderine (with a picture on it), and Skitterine (small and bouncy), a nickname the family used for Angela herself.

She began to read, and at five and a half was given her first book, Mrs Trimmer's *History of the Robins*,* which was in words of one syll-a-ble, but sophisticated nevertheless. She developed the urge to draw and paint and spent her pocket money on brushes. Significantly her drawings were of babies and children, and no doubt she christened those too.

*Preserved in Coventry City Library.

FRIENDS AND A FIRE

The ritual of Sunday reverence continued to bore her. The
Brazils attended St John's Church, which was close to their house,
and the services seemed interminable; morning prayer, litany,
ante-communion, and a long, dry, incomprehensible sermon. The
clergyman preached in a black gown and black kid gloves, but he
was not so absorbed as to overlook Angela building castles with
hymn-books in the square, cushioned pew. Demonstrating a nice
self-awareness, Angela commented: 'With my intensely romantic
disposition I fancy a short, *very*, short musical service in a "dim
religious light" of stained-glass windows and ancient pillars might
have appealed to me.' What *did* appeal to her were the burnt ruins
behind Wallesey Church (covered with ivy, of course) where she
would cajole the housemaid, Anne, to take her on their walks. One
winter afternoon, sunny after a sudden thaw, she witnessed the
funeral of a local boy who had drowned by falling through the ice.
Angela and Anne sat on a flat tombstone among the crowd, and
Anne cried. Clergy and choristers, dressed in white and singing
'Jerusalem my Happy Home', passed in procession on their way
into the church. Angela had never seen surplices before. She
thought the boys looked like angels. Expectancy gave way to a
numinous sense she had failed to experience in the puritan
austerity of St John's, and, she said, it awakened her. 'At home I
was taught about heaven and angels. But that was teaching. This
was something different – something I had seen for myself.'
She responded to the mystic in religion just as she responded to the
mysteries of the sea and the mythology of fairy-lore. (There is a thesis
to be written on Angela Brazil's obsession with the world of faery.)
At six and a half she was sent to school to The Turrets in
Wallasey (a name she utilized sixty years later in *The School at The
Turrets*) which was not unlike the dame-school she had attended
in Preston for that one brief morning. The Misses Allison replaced
the sisters Knowles, teaching being a customary pursuit of genteel
ladies in straitened circumstances.

> Miss Allison and her sister Fanny were ladies of great refine-
> ment and beautiful speech and manners, but their sole idea of
> educating a girl was to put a book in her hand, set her a portion
> to learn by heart, and hear her recite it when she knew it. That
> was all!

Angela learned *The Wreck of the Hesperus, The Burial of Sir
John Moore, We Are Seven* and many other verses from the
volumes of *Selections for the Young*, which was a sound training for

B   33

the compulsory learning required of her at Ellerslie. She loved to declaim the horror and tragedy, and won a prize for her efforts, a curious book called *The Covetous Man*, in which a poor but beautiful girl was married to a rich, irreligious husband, who ill-treated her, took to drink and died unrepentant. Less successful were Angela's attempts at arithmetic; there was a fracas over the seven times table, in which Amy was reprimanded severely for defending her sister's right not to learn, an episode which was re-enacted in *Schoolgirl Kitty*:

'You *shan't* learn your tables,' she said, wildly angry, and threw the book out of the window.

She also had difficulty in sitting silent, upright and still. She conceived a loathing for an innocently good child called Tetta (the prototype for many a 'goody-goody' in 'the works') and a love for Effie, a boarder.

The very fact of *being* a boarder gave Effie an added attraction. The garden at The Turrets was reserved for boarders (although Angela made swift, secret tours of it); there was a special privilege in being away from home, a choice fate which Angela tasted only minimally when she boarded in a hostel during her last year at Ellerslie and which she always envied. Day-girls were to her mind inferior to boarders, a prejudice she never overcame.

'The fact is, she's here, and I suppose we can't get rid of her,' admitted Irma.

'After all, she's a boarder!' ventured Ethelberga.

'Only a weekly one,' qualified Janet.

'And a Hawthorner!' added Laura.

'She said she hadn't been to school since last Christmas,' commented Ethelberga.

'Why, so she did! Then she's had a sort of break from The Hawthorns, and in a way she's making a fresh start here.'

'I suppose so.'

'If she'd be loyal to Silverside, though we could never like her, we might bring ourselves to tolerate her.'

'A boarder's a boarder!'

When the girls returned to the Cowslip Room, they found their new companion with emptied box putting the last of her possessions into her drawers.

'Look here, Avelyn Watson,' said Laura. 'We've been talking you over. Although you go home for the weekend, you're still a boarder, and at Silverside boarders are a very different thing from day girls, as you'll soon find out. If you've had two whole terms away from those Hawthorners, just forget them, and consider yourself entirely one of us. If you do that, we'll count you on our side; but if you've anything to do with day girls, we'll cut you dead.'

'I don't quite understand,' returned Avelyn.

'You soon will!' said Janet significantly.

'I advise you to think it over,' added Laura.*

Effie, the boarder, no doubt envied Angela, the day-girl. Angela flung herself into the friendship with a passion that was characteristic, and insisted that they must share equally; kisses from the adults were counted jealously (Effie spent most Saturdays at Angela's house) and on Angela's seventh birthday, Effie had a cake too. The sense of betrayal that Angela endured when Effie rejected her for Hilda is the kernel of Isobel Stewart's disillusionment in *Bosom Friends*. From the intensity of *A Hot Friendship* (Ch. 5) to the disappointment in *Belle's New Friend* (Ch. 16) Angela charted her first experience of love's labours lost.

If it ever struck her that her companion was lacking in some of those qualities which she had been taught to consider necessary, she thrust the thought away as a kind of disloyalty; and if it were she who generally carried the heavy basket, searched for the lost ball, fetched for forgotten articles, or did any of the countless small services which Belle exacted almost as a matter of course from those around her, it certainly was without any idea of complaint. There are in this world always those who love and those who are loved, and Isobel was ready with spendthrift generosity to offer her utmost in way of friendship, finding Belle's pretty thanks and kisses a sufficient reward for any trouble she might take on her account, and perhaps unconsciously realizing that even in our affections it is the givers more than the receivers who are truly blessed.

Effie, careless of the love offered her by Angela, innocently begat a series of fictional 'hot friendships' that flamed and cooled and were replaced. From the odiously smug and snobbish Maud Middleton in *A Terrible Tomboy*,† who was a pencil sketch for the

---

* *For the School Colours.*

† 'We're going to London next week,' drawled Maud in her most grown-up manner, 'we've taken a house in Mayfair. Mother always likes to go up for a while during the season. We've so many friends, don't you know.'

portrait of Belle, to Regina's jealous obsession in *Loyal to the School*, Angela continually externalized her agony over Effie. She was a demanding friend, and she did not forgive.

While she was being tested by the barometer of Effie's friendship, another kind of relationship was being established, as far reaching in its effect. In fact, together, Effie's cavalier behaviour and a new-found passion for mothering little children probably accounted for Angela's fixation over schoolgirls. I am not a psychologist and would not want to make a categorical claim, but the insecurity Effie introduced into Angela's hitherto untroubled world could have been more damaging than Angelica ever imagined. 'In my disappointment,' said Angela, 'I wept and wept and wept until my eyes were red slits and my cheeks were sore.' That blow to the ego, the feeling of being unwanted by a chosen contemporary, was enough to direct future friendships into safer areas – areas where seniority was tacitly acknowledged.

The Misses Allison possessed several small nieces who came to stay at The Turrets, and thus Angela discovered the satisfaction of unquestioned superiority.

> One was a darling four-year-old to whom I took an immense liking. She passed much of her time sitting on my lap in the schoolroom, where my fairy stories kept both of us happy and out of mischief. I turned 'little teacher', and taught her to make pot-hooks, and repeat scraps of poetry. To be allowed to curl her hair was a supreme reward for good behaviour. I was outrageously angry when she was put in the corner once, and proud of her cleverness when she employed her time of punishment there by licking the wallpaper! I wanted to keep her! She made me long for a small sister of my own. But such luck never came my way. I don't suppose anybody at home wanted to start up another nursery. *Some*body had to finish up a family and remain youngest.

Angela not only remained the youngest but, as she constantly pointed out, a schoolgirl at heart. She scarcely moved out of the Brazil nursery, spending much time with her mother (until Angelica's death in 1915) and her indulgent elder sister and brother Walter until she herself died (the first of the three) in 1947. She had only two close external friendships, one of which began in her schooldays and the other in her late thirties. Both friends were schoolgirls when the relationships began. The pleasure and security she found in tending and bossing the Allison nieces was reiterated in life and in many of the books, but never more explicitly than in *The School in the South*, published in 1922.

The 'south' was Fossato, a small town close to Naples, and the 'high class boarding-school' the Villa Camellia, where the two new girls, senior Irene Beverly and junior Désirée Legrand (nicknamed 'Little Flaxen' by Irene) were attempting to settle in. Irene overcame her problems by producing a box of chocolates. ('Instantly all were chumping almonds, and the icy atmosphere thawed into summer. "Don't I bless Dad for those chocs!" she thought as she took her seat at a desk. "They worked the trick. If I'd had nothing to offer that crew I might have sat out in the cold for evermore."') Désirée was less well equipped to cope and Irene found her 'squatting forlornly on the steps that led to the upper tennis courts' and mopping her eyes for lack of love. After a brisk pep talk ('Can't you brace up and be sporty?') Irene offered a solution. 'Why don't you write home for a box of chocs and offer them round your form?' Désirée skipped off happily, but Irene found that she was brooding about the maltreated junior. When she learned that *other* juniors were being persecuted by the malicious girls of the Transition, she called a meeting of the Camellia Buds, a secret society devoted to friendship, and described how the Transition had appropriated the daily allowance of biscuits.

'Poor little souls, it's a sneaking rag to prig their "bikkies", we'll have to stand over them and act fairy godmothers,' said Sheila.

Peachy bounced suddenly in her seat.

'Sheila Yonge, you've given me an idea – yes, an absolute brain-throb. What the Camellia Buds ought to do is to turn the sorority into an Amalgamated Society of Fairy Godmothers, and each of us take over a junior to look after and act providence to. It's what those kids are just aching for – only they mayn't know it. What good are prefects to them except as bogies? They skedaddle like lightening if they so much as see Rachel's shadow. They each ought to have one older girl whom they can count on as a friend.'

'A kind of buddy?'

'Something of the sort, but more like a foster mother.'

'I vote we ask them all to a candy party, and each adopt one,' suggested Delia warmly.

'There are ten of us, and there are nineteen juniors,' calculated Jess. 'How's it going to work out?'

'Why, some of us must take twins or even triplets,' decreed
Peachy. 'I'm bursting to begin. Let's have the candy party right
away. Can anybody raise a lira or two?'

Lire were raised, the 'goodies' acquired and distributed to
'sticky satisfaction', and the Camellia Buds explained their
proposition. Agnes, the spokeswoman, 'held up her hand to stop
the general clamour'.

'I'm going to sort you out and give you each to your fairy
godmother, and you may pour your woes into her ears, and
she'll try her level best to right your wrongs. No, you *mayn't* say
whom you'd like to have. It's *we* who'll do the choosing,
thanks! Anybody who's not satisfied can walk off, and she won't
get a champion at all or any more candy either.'

I cannot help wondering if Angela herself resorted to sweet-
meats in times of stress, she had such faith in their compensatory
value. The candy party at the Villa Camellia bought loyalty as well
as content.

'The seniors gave us a simply top-hole time,' confided
Désirée to Irene afterwards. 'We'd cream-puffs and almond
biscuits and preserved ginger, and we played games for prizes.
But don't think we liked it any better than your candy parties.
The prefects are awfully kind to us now, but it was you who
took us up *first*! We can't forget *that*!'

Angela acquired the gratitude and loyalty of several generations
of children (predominantly girls) in Llanbedr, Coventry and
Cornwall where she fed them lavishly and sweetly at the renowned
parties, more lavishly than some of her adult guests who have
hinted of frugality at the Brazil board. Seduction by confec-
tionery, together with the other ingredients which make Angela
Brazil's early school stories so memorable (the slang, the implicit
moral lessons, the literary allusions, the understanding of the shy
child), were perfectly combined in Chapter One (*Off to Boarding
School*) of *A Patriotic Schoolgirl*.

'Dona, are you awake? Donakins! I say, old sport, do stir
yourself and blink an eye! What a dormouse you are! D'you
want shaking? Rouse up, you old bluebottle, can't you?'
'I've been awake since five o'clock, and it's no use thumping

me in the back,' grunted an injured voice from the next bed. 'It's too early yet to get up, and I wish you'd leave me alone.'

The huskiness and general chokiness of the tone were unmistakable. Marjorie leaned over and took a keen survey of that portion of her sister's face which was not buried in the pillow.

'Oh! the atmosphere's damp, is it?' she remarked. 'Dona, you're ostriching! For goodness' sake brace up, child, and turn off the water-works! I thought you'd more pluck. If you're going to arrive at Brackenfield with a red nose and your eyes all bunged up, I'll disown you or lose you on the way. Crystal clear, I will! I'll not let you start in a new school nicknamed "Niobe", so there! Have a caramel?'

Dona sat up in bed, and arrested her tears sufficiently to accept the creature comfort offered her. As its consistency was decidedly of a stick-jaw nature, the mingled sucking and sobbing which followed produced a queer combination.

'You sound like a seal at the zoo,' Marjorie assured her airily. 'Cheer oh! I call it a stunt to be going to Brackenfield. I mean to have a top-hole time there, and no mistake!'

'It's all very well for you!' sighed Dona dolefully. 'You've been at boarding school before, and I haven't; and you are not shy, and you always get on with people. You know I'm a mum mouse, and I hate strangers. I shall endure till the holidays come. It's no use telling me to brace up, for there's nothing to brace about.'

Angela remembered the three and a half years at Egremont as a period of excitement, development and growth, but she probably did not realize that she drew from it the life-blood of her work. Not only were the foundations laid for her future friendships, limiting them in scope and giving her the material for her 'girls', but a combination of experience and interest provided her with the four elements that influenced the schematic structure of all her books. The analogy of the elements is not far-fetched. There was earth (the botany); there was air (the folklore, mythology, idealism and romance); there was water (all that shipwrecking and detailed seascape); and there was fire, which excited her visually and gave her inspiration for acts of bravery which excelled all others faced by her heroines.

One marvellous sight I witnessed in my childhood – the burning of the Liverpool landing-stage. I had gone to bed when my father returned home with news of the fire (he had reached Egremont with difficulty). And later I was taken up and dressed and went out with the rest of my family to watch the spectacle. How vividly I remember it! Moonlight shone over the great wide estuary, and on the far side opposite glared a long, long line of red, from which flames shot up, casting a lurid gleam on the water, in utter contrast to the white light of the moon-beams . . . Never shall I forget the effect of leaping fire and My Lady Moon riding tranquilly overhead.

Not long afterwards a second fire occurred when a Liverpool factory burst into flames, and added fuel to her own imagery. It was a scene, she said, 'in which a Turner would have revelled', and the conflagration was the source for the fire at Birkwood,* when Aldred was able to prove herself and her friendship for Mabel in the face of death by burning, and it is such a splendid example of Angela's work that it must be quoted at length. Here are the final pages of the chapter entitled *An Opportunity*.

Aldred grasped the fact only too speedily that there was but one terrible answer to her question. *Mabel was in the burning house, for nobody had gone to warn her*. Without a moment's hesitation, she rushed back to the front door. There was no alternative; the emergency was all-compelling. Mabel was in imminent and pressing danger; no one realised it, or had even missed her, and there was no time to appeal to Miss Forster or Miss Bardsley. She, Aldred, alone and on her own responsi-bility, must save her friend. There was not a second to be lost; already it might be too late, for the blaze was fast making headway. From the open door clouds of smoke belched forth as if from a furnace, and Aldred was driven back with blinded eyes choking and gasping for breath. It was her own fault. How stupid she was to forget, in her excitement, what she had learned at the fire-drill practice! Her dripping pocket-handkerchief was still clasped, almost unconsciously, in her hand; she tied it rapidly over her nose and mouth, then, dropping on to her hands and knees, she began to crawl along the hall in the direc-tion of the staircase. The difference was marvellous. Down on the ground the air was comparatively fresh and clear – she could see the bottom of the umbrella stand and a pair of Miss Drum-mond's galoshes quite plainly; while only a foot higher the atmosphere was dense and impenetrable. The wet handkerchief

* in *A Fourth Form Friendship*.

also made breathing easier, and though her eyes were smarting and the heat was very great, she found it quite possible to get along. With half-closed eyelids, and her mouth well to the floor, she crept up the stairs; each one seemed a victory gained, and a step nearer to the accomplishment of her purpose. Oh, how many there were, and how interminable was the passage at the top! The heat grew more intense, and a roaring, crackling sound warned her that she was reaching the west wing, where the flames were raging worst and had burst through the windows.

The hospital was on the top storey, so there was another staircase to be mounted. Dare she do it? Every step cut off her retreat, and put another bar between her and safety. Yet Mabel was there, solitary, unaided, in the midst of awful peril. No, she could not abandon her, come what might! She would face death with her friend, rather than leave her to perish alone.

She never remembered quite how she dragged herself along; her nerves were strung to the highest pitch, her brain felt bursting. The room she was in search of was over the kitchen, where the fire had originally broken out. Fortunately, it was a little clearer there, and Aldred was able to stand up; and by groping her way along the walls, she found the handle and flung open the door of the hospital.

'Mabel! Mabel!' she cried vehemently. There was no reply. The room was filled with smoke, but the glare outside made just enough light to distinguish objects.

'Mabel! Are you there? Mabel!'

Aldred was in an agony of apprehension. There were several beds in the hospital, and she ran from one to the other, feeling in them with eager hands. They were empty. Had she, after all, come on a vain quest? Mabel must have heard the alarm bell, and have escaped and joined the others in the garden! Aldred's heart almost stopped beating, as for a moment the horror of the situation overcame her. Her search was quixotic, fruitless – she had risked her life for nothing! She moved instinctively to clutch a bed-post to steady herself, and as she did so her foot touched something soft. With a cry she dropped on her knees. Mabel was lying on the floor just by the bedside, where she must have fallen, overpowered by the smoke, in an effort to make her way to the door.

With frantic hands Aldred dragged her friend across the room, and by sheer effort of will hoisted her up, so that her head might reach the open window. It was a task far beyond her ordinary powers, but in such moments a strength not our own is often given to us. The fresh air soon restored consciousness, and Mabel, to Aldred's intense relief, opened her eyes.

'What is it? Where am I?' she asked confusedly.

'The house is on fire, dear, and I don't know how we are to save ourselves. Stay where you are, and go on getting the air; I'm going to see if we can manage to get back down the passage.'

Directly Aldred opened the door she realized that escape in that quarter was impossible. A roaring sound and a glare at the end of the landing told her only too plainly that the staircase had broken into flames. She shut the door again hurriedly, and, returning to the window, shouted with all her might. Would anybody hear, and if so, could they help? The Fire Brigade had not yet arrived from Chetbourne, and it was unlikely that there would be any ladder about the place long enough to reach the top storey of the house.

'Help! Help! Hallo!' Her voice sounded so thin and weak, compared with the crackling of the flames, she feared it would not carry far enough. Mabel, still in a half-dazed state, clung to her wildly, trembling and shivering with terror.

Would no one ever come? They were all watching the front of the house, and had completely forgotten the back.

At last! There was a shout from below, and a sudden rushing and noise, as the ever-increasing crowd poured round the corner.

'Fetch a ladder!'

'It's too short!'

'Tie two together!'

'There aren't two!'

'Tell them to jump!'

'No! No! They'd break their necks!'

'Someone go in and fetch 'em!'

'Impossible! The stairs are ablaze!'

'Does anyone hear the engine coming?'

'Not a sign of it yet!'

'Then God help them, for we can't!'

The room was getting hotter and hotter. Aldred could hear the roar of the flames in the passage now. How long would the door keep them out? It was plain that, unless both girls were to perish, something must be done, and that instantly. Disengaging Mabel's clinging arms, Aldred propped her against the window-sill, then groped her way through the dense smoke across the room. The six beds in the hospital were always kept made up, perfectly ready for use. Aldred pulled off the twelve sheets one after the other, and carried them in a bundle back to the window, where, with trembling hands, she knotted them firmly together, just as Miss Drummond had shown in the fire-drill practice. She dragged forward the nearest bedstead till its foot almost touched the sill, and, fastening her improvised rope round a post, pulled it hard, to make sure that the knot was safe.

'Mabel,' she said loudly, 'we must try the sheet dodge. I'm going to lower you down. Let me tie this end round your waist, quick!'

'No! No!' cried Mabel, who had somewhat recovered her scattered senses. 'I'll lower you! I'm the bigger, and stronger than you. Here, give me the end!'

'I shan't. You must go! Mabel, I insist! This is no time for arguing. My mind's made up, and I shall make you!'

Aldred was fastening the knot as she spoke, with quick fingers. She would take no denial. Had she not come to rescue her friend, and was she to be so easily gainsaid?

'But, Aldred! Aldred! If I go first, who will lower you afterwards?'

'I'll slip down somehow.'

'You know you can't! It's saving me at your own cost!'

The heat was terrific, and the roar on the landing had increased sevenfold. With a crash the door fell in, and a sheet of flame burst like a furious living thing into the room.

Aldred turned almost fiercely upon Mabel.

'For your father's and mother's sake! Think of them.'

Her nature was the stronger and the more masterful of the two. She had always been the dominating influence, and now, in this great and awful crisis, her will prevailed. Without further ado she pushed Mabel over the window-sill, and, clinging with all her might to the sheet rope, let her down as carefully and gently as she could. It was a great effort to regulate the descent of such a heavy dangling weight, but she feared to let her burden go with a run, lest Mabel's head should be dashed against the wall of the house. Oh, what a fearful, dizzy depth it seemed from the upper storey to the ground! The crowd below stood stock-still, pressed tightly together shoulder to shoulder, and gazing upward, voiceless and almost breathless with suspense. Would Aldred's frail strength accomplish the task?

The fire within had gained a grip of the room, and shone behind her head like a halo. Still she did not flinch or falter; she kept her nerve, and paid out her rope piece by piece, manoeuvring the knots over the window-sill, and remembering every necessary precaution.

The flames rolled nearer. Strangely enough, now that death was almost at arm's length, she felt perfectly cool and collected, and far calmer than she had done when first she had entered the room. Every thought and effort of her being was concentrated on Mabel's escape; after that she cared nothing. Only a few yards now! She set her teeth, and hung on grimly. She was nearly spent, but she just managed to control the last quick rush as the rope's burden fell at length into the dozen eager hands upraised to help. The crowd had waited in silence, but now a roar rose up from below of deafening cheers and loud shouts of encouragement.

'Come down yourself!'

'Try hand over hand down the sheets!'

'Don't waste a minute!'

'Pluck will win yet!'

'We're all waiting to catch you if you fall!'

But Aldred, standing exhausted and panting by the window, had no strength left for further effort. The heat of the flames and the smoke were overpowering. She had kept up by sheer effort of will until her friend was in safety; now the world seemed suddenly to be turning round her. There was a rushing in her ears, and her eyes grew dim. Through a thick haze she saw the crowd beckoning to her, and one man, more daring than the rest, began to scale the rope, in the hope of rescuing her. He could never reach her in time, she thought vaguely; and she was too faint and giddy to let herself down hand over hand, as they were calling to her to do. She almost wished they would leave her alone; her work was done, Mabel was safe, and that was all she cared.

Why was the crowd suddenly turning round and hurrahing? The people were breaking up in wild confusion, and parting so as to leave a wide path in their midst. There were sounds of galloping horses and grinding wheels. What did it all mean? Aldred's fading senses just grasped a vision of men in bright helmets, of a great ladder that seemed to advance faster than the wind, and of a tongue of flame that shot out from the room behind and enveloped her, and the fact that a strong arm at the same instant clutched her and snatched her away; then she went down – down – down, and everything sank into blank nothingness.

But the crowd below cried: 'Thank God! The fire brigade came in the nick of time!'

[4]
LOYALTY

'I remember an incipient friendship which I was fated to miss', wrote Angela forty years after the event – after the *non*-event, in fact. It is remarkable that the relationship that never was should continue to create a sense of loss. Perhaps those many pairings (Isobel and Isabelle; Aldred and Mabel; Dona and Alison; Lorna and Irene; Alison and Dorothy – a random selection from the blossoming hundreds) were created in recompense for a little girl in a pony carriage who smiled at Angela Brazil.

She had no soul-mate in Egremont. The family was not sufficient. In spite of her protestations that it was not so, the older Brazils indulged her, and from the security of her home the baby of the household yearned for a friendship in which she was the prime giver. Hadn't Angelica, on Angela's birthday and on Angela's insistence, made a birthday cake for Effie too?

Leaving Liverpool increased Angela's need. The well-to-do suburb of Greenhayes in Manchester, no doubt a social step in the right direction, was to her a poor replacement for Merseyside.

> To us young folks at any rate it was a matter of great regret. We had loved the estuary of the Mersey, with its shining grey expanse of water, its tides, its gleaming sands, its shipping, its sense of space and light, its touch with the infinite sea, its whisper of foreign countries, and its lonely sandhills, where the sweet-scented little yellow wild roses grew in June. Oh, it was hard to say goodbye to all that.

The three senior offspring suffered less than nine-year-old Angela. The boys were practically grown up, Walter was studying medicine at the university, Clarence law. Amy, at fifteen, was immediately absorbed into the busy life of Manchester High School, but Angela, separated not only from the open spaces but from Amy's daily protection, endured a real sense of isolation.

She was sent to the Preparatory High. Dressed in the uniform coat and hat of tweed edged with scarlet satin, she revelled in the ambience and appurtenances of a 'proper' school, but there was no one she felt able to ask home to tea. One detects the hints of snobbishness which sowed the seeds of Angela's own. Angelica did not approve of her daughter's new classroom companions, indeed she ultimately removed her from the school because of them. *Their* mothers allowed them to run along the pavements and buy sweets from the local shops, *they* behaved with a 'perkiness' which Angela soon began to acquire, a manner the Brazils associated with the *nouveau riche*. Did Angelica curb enthusiasm in the manner of Aunt Helen in *A Terrible Tomboy*? 'But, my dear child, you have not yet told me who she is. I cannot have you making friends with any shopkeeper's daughter.' Possibly it was in self-defence that Angela began to build her fantasies around the 'dear little girl' who occasionally drove by the house in the pony trap. 'She always looked at me,' Angela recalled, 'and poked her mother eagerly, then turned and smiled at me. I grew to watch for the pony trap when I went for my walks.'

One morning Amy awoke with the measles. Angelica was out on a district charity visit when the doctor confirmed the complaint, and the maids, at a loss to occupy Angela, sent her out with the warning that she might be infectious too.

I ran till I was tired of bowling my hoop, and then I stood still. Suddenly, from the opposite side of the road, alone, quite alone, danced my dear little girl, and greeted me with wild enthusiasm. She was waiting for her mother! How delightful to meet me! What was my name? And a dozen other quick eager questions with no pause in between.

And I! I was too staggered to find words! I who was generally ready enough with my tongue, seemed possessed by a dumb demon! The whole fact of the matter was that I feared I was 'infectious'. Conscience urged me hotly to tell her that Amy was in bed with measles, and that I also was probably a leper, with whom she ought not to converse. I managed indeed to gasp forth my name, but I was still shilly-shallying with my confession when up drove the pony trap. My radiant little friend turned and entered. She smiled and waved a fairy hand, and her

47

mother smiled, and I gave an embarrassed half-hearted smile, which did not convey the real warmth of my feelings. I could have loved that child.

Loved! Throughout her written accounts of friendships, whether her own or fictional, Angela used terms which generally relate to the romantic love of adults. Take Irene, 'love-lorn' for Peachy in *The School in the South*, for instance. 'She's just sweet to me, but I don't count first,' she told herself. 'Well, it's no use being jealous. If you can't have the moon you must be content with a star.' The star was Lorna, and Lorna 'adored' Irene. Then there was Dona Anderson's 'immensely hot' friendship with Ailsa in *A Patriotic Schoolgirl*; 'they spent every available moment of the day together.' In *The Fortunes of Philippa* the heroine announced, 'I've simply fallen in love with Catherine Winstanley,' and as for Aldred and Mabel, whose friendship was complicated from the outset, their final scene after the traumatic drama of the fire reads like the closing pages of a novelette.

'I'd have given my life for you gladly!' gulped Aldred.
'I know, and I feel almost unworthy of such love.'
'Will you kiss me, to show you can forget what's past?'
Mabel bent her head. It was a kiss of complete reconciliation and forgiveness, and Aldred, with a glad leap of her heart, felt that the friendship that she had striven to build upon the shifting sand of a false reputation was founded at last upon the rock of self-sacrifice and human endeavour.

An astrologer once told Angela that Saturn's intrusion into her horoscope was an unfortunate influence on friendship and love. 'Certainly,' she said of the girl in the pony carriage, 'he popped in a baleful finger,' and she continued to cherish that unfulfilled fervour as a Lost Opportunity.

Such episodes, stored in the mental archives, emerged in The Works. Isobel's first glimpse of Isabelle at the station en route for Silversands must surely have its origin in the waver of the fairy hand, 'a little girl of about her own age, a child who appeared so charmingly pretty to Isobel's eyes that she could not help gazing at her in scarcely-concealed admiration'. That the beautiful ringletted and beribboned Belle turned out to have the disposition of disloyal Effie was yet another of Angela's compensations for a childhood disappointment when reality fell short of dreams.

Con was not a figment of the imagination. She was by no means the perfect chum – Angela found her later – but she sufficed for the time being, temporarily assuaging the thirst for friendship. Angelica approved; Con's mother was an acquaintance, her father a doctor; even more important she counteracted the influence of the pupils from the Preparatory High, and if she did not share Angela's fascination for fairy stories, they had other things in common. Con was an adventurous, cheerful child, fond of practical jokes and practical pursuits. They dressed up and convinced Con's mother that they were from the domestic agency, or so Angela believed, although it seems unlikely that the midget pair were really so credible. They visited Con's parents' farm, riding there in a phaeton behind Amy and Con's elder brother and sister on ponies. Literary Angela, with her stock of poems from The Turrets, thought of herself as John Gilpin as they forded the river to the countryside. When they were there they played in the fields, picked primroses and looked for birds' nests. Angela remembered eating new laid eggs and honey for tea 'in a rather musty little sitting room', the kind of wholesome tea her heroines often consumed. She also, for the first time, inaugurated a Secret Society, of which she and Con were the sole members. Its purpose was to invent games and record them in a specially purchased notebook, which they contrived to do behind the locked nursery door.

Secrecy was the essence of enjoyment for Angela, even when secrecy was unnecessary. 'We vow to be loyal to one another and to our president and never reveal the secrets of our society,' swear the members of the Starry Circle, in *The School in the South*.

'Will you give your word of honour to be a loyal member of the Sorority of Camellia Buds, and never do a dirty trick as long as you remain in this school?' asked the masked figure in the dormitory in the same book.

'Look here!' said Verity in *A Popular Schoolgirl*, 'If we want to have a jolly term we four must stick together. Let's make a compact that, both in school and in the hostel we'll support each other through thick and thin. We'll be a sort of society of Freemasons. I haven't made up any secrets yet, but whoever betrays them will be outlawed! Let's call ourselves "The Foursome League". Now then, put your right hands all together on mine, and say after me: "I hereby promise and vow on my honour as a gentlewoman that I'll stand by my chums in No. 2 Dormitory at any cost."'

'I've found out from Miss Duckworth,' [said Mrs Morrison, Principal of Brackenfield in *A Patriotic Schoolgirl*] 'that you have founded a secret society among yourselves for the purpose of encouraging patriotism. I do not in general approve of secret societies, but I sympathise with your object.'

'What shall we call our society?' asked Dulcie [in *The Princess of the School*].
'There's a big secret society in Sicily called "The Mafia",' vouchsafed Carmel.
'Then let us call ours "The Chilcombe Mafia"...when things get bad, "The Mafia" will take them up.'
'Strike secretly and suddenly,' agreed Dulcie with a chuckle.

And Millie, in *The Little Green School*, asks: 'What's the society going to be called? How would The Fair Play Union do?'
It did, of course, extremely well, because Angela was a strong supporter of fair play and inculcated its principles whenever she had the opportunity. In *My Own Schooldays* she wrote:

One thing for which I always stood up was fair play and equality. School, in my opinion, was a commonwealth where all were entitled to equal chances, and any suspicion of favouritism, especially of awarding popularity to a girl on the basis of her father's wealth instead of her own claims, invariably aroused my strongest antagonism. What a girl was at home mattered nothing; it was the school aspect of her that counted, and at that valuation I insisted she should be taken.

If one practised fair play, it went without saying that one was loyal; loyal to one's family (particularly to one's mother); loyal to one's friends, one's school, one's headmistress and, of course, one's country.
Fathers, who play an ambivalent role in the Brazil novels, were generally brave, even when wronged, and always loyal to their ideals. Lorna's father (his honour falsely ruined by the father of her best friend) did not hesitate for a moment when the man who had injured him was inside the cavern, perhaps in deadly danger, and he was going to risk his own life and his daughter's to save him.
Such British and heroic gestures were true to Angela's concept of the male. They were noble in mind but undemonstrative to

their daughters. It was always the mothers who interceded and broke the news of failing family fortunes. 'Poor little woman,' said Mrs Saxon to Ingrid, who had taken the news badly in *A Popular Schoolgirl*,

> 'Remember it's just as hard for all the rest of us. We've each got a burden to carry at present. Suppose we see who can be pluckiest over it. We're fighting fortune now, instead of the Hun, and we must show a brave face. Won't you march with the family regiment, and keep the colours flying?'

Clarence Brazil – and we know very little about him – was no typical *pater-familias*, but he did not actively involve himself with his children. He saw his duty as provider and religious instructor; he teased his daughters in a rather ludicrous and irritating manner if the examples given by Angela are typical; he never attempted to talk to them at their own level, or to play with them.

Angela, always aware of social changes affecting the young, regretted that in her youth she had no adult friends. The one exception was Con's father's assistant who bought her a pound of sweets and won a doll for her at a church bazaar. It was a French doll, made of china, with glass eyes and fair pigtails and a pink silk dress. She kept it, and when she died Amy gave it to the Herbert Museum together with other treasures in the collection Angela had kept in the glass-fronted case in her Boudoir.

In the collection of fathers, quite as permanently preserved, the most extraordinary is Mr Carrington* in *Schoolgirl Kitty*, who, in his passion for advancement (inadvertently foiled by Kitty) had a 'bitterness in his voice' which 'struck cold as iron'; pushing Kitty aside, he ordered his wife, 'Send her to the nursery – anywhere out of my sight! I tell you I can't bear to look at her! She's spoilt my life.' Kitty, naturally, was loyal to him.

There is not a harsh mother anywhere. The only disinterest was displayed by Mrs Meredith in *Nesta's New School*, but she wasn't Nesta's real mother, who, reunited with her daughter, demonstrated the affection to which Angela's heroines are accustomed.

> 'You've come from Switzerland? From the Villa Alpina?'
> 'Yes.'
> 'Then, my darling child, let me give you a kiss. I'm your mother.'

---

* The surname Angela used more than once as an alias for Brazil.

Angela's friendship with Con was curtailed by yet another household move. Urban life was encroaching too fast upon Green-hayes for the country-loving Brazils, and only eighteen months after arriving there, they began to look for a new house. Possibly the proximity of Ellerslie, the most select school in Manchester, determined the exact choice of location. Rusholme was a mere ten minutes away from the esteemed neighbourhood of Victoria Park, where Angela might find suitable friends. They had been there less than a week when an invitation from the children of a local clergy-man to a birthday tea changed her life.

There was another guest when Angela arrived. Her name was Leila Langdale, she was ten years old and she took one look at Angela's curls and thought: 'That girl is conceited.' Angela, introduced, took an instant dislike to Leila's silver locket and said to herself: 'That child is vain.' They sat at either end of the drawing-room sofa, and when they were taken upstairs to the nursery they did not speak a word. Half an hour later they had become enrapt, and by the end of the afternoon they had cemented a friendship that was to last for life. 'If human beings have auras, hers and mine must have instantly mixed.'

It was an approach to the mysterious and powerful quality of friendship that Angela never relinquished. Auras and souls reach forth and mingle in mystic recognition in classroom, home and dormitory as girl finds girl in book after book. 'As a rule we can't deliberately choose our soul-friends,' the author comments in *The School in the South*.

> 'Occasionally in our lives we meet with people whose whole electric atmosphere seems to merge and blend with our own. We feel we are not so much making a new acquaintance as picking up the lost threads of some former soul-friendship.'*

Invisible bonds draw together members of the female sex in implicit understanding and uncompromising love. 'We had dove-tailed into each other's grooves', said Angela of her meeting with Leila, 'and might have been chums for years.'

As with Con, parental approval placed the seal. Both Leila's mother and Angelica were delighted that their youngest children had formed the attachment and arranged for them to play together every weekend. Their houses were only a few doors apart, and Angela could signal to Leila from bedroom to garden by a secret

* *For the School Colours.*

code. She drew a picture of her new friend, painted it in water-
colours with great care and called it *Leila in her plum-coloured dress
and pinafore*. Their characters were complementary; Angela daring
and imaginative, Leila gentle, patient, but ready to follow. Later
Leila emerged as Lilian in *A Terrible Tomboy*, counterpart to
Angela's Peggy. The story, of course, is an amalgam; the other
children were Leila's own, the adventures drawn from both
generations; Lilian was (for reasons of plot) older than her sister
Peggy; the dog, Rollo, was a Collie owned by the Brazils in
Egremont; but the setting, Llanbedr in North Wales, was one that
the Brazils and Langdales shared, and which Angela, Amy and
Leila continued to share when they had all grown up. In later life
(schoolgirl-like) Angela made a list of her friends and their
'virtues' to be 'copied and admired'! She listed Leila's as 'pleasant-
ness and wide interests'. If we are to take Lilian as Leila's true
portrait, then in childhood her disposition must have been anxious,
sweet and slightly melancholic.

When quite a tiny child she had much preferred the tragedy
of Red Riding Hood to the brighter fate of the princesses who
lived happily ever afterwards, and, with the tears streaming
down her fat little cheeks, would quaver out 'Tell it again!' Her
first efforts in poetry had been in a distinctly pensive strain.
When only about nine years old she had composed –

The Dying Child's Last Words
'Remember me when I am gone,
And me thou canst not see;
When I lie sleeping in my grave,
Dear friends, remember me.

'You'll keep my little garden neat,
My clothes you'll fold away;
My playthings in a drawer you'll put
With which I last did play.'

Whose poem, Lilian's – or Leila's? So much from those first
books is autobiographical, including verses, and Lilian's strain of
sadness cannot have been far removed from the actuality of Leila's
feelings. Her mother died when she was in her teens, her father
soon afterwards, and she took on the responsibility of running the
home as Lilian had to do in *A Terrible Tomboy*, and as Kitty
Carrington did in *Schoolgirl Kitty*, finely balancing the dual
stresses of school and domestic demands. There were financial

setbacks, too, and while Angela was enjoying art school in London, Leila took a post as a nursery governess, facts which influenced Angela's attitudes to true worth and monetary status. It seems highly probable that Lesbia Ferrar's experiences as a holiday governess in *Loyal to the School* had their basis in Leila's own. As Lesbia set off by train, true to Brazil psychology she 'ate her chocolates to try to banish the uneasy forebodings' at the prospect of coping with young Terry Stockton, 'equal mixture of angel and elf', a description that is unmistakably from Angela's whimsical pen. The subsequent stress in controlling the ebullient energy of her charge has the ring of reality that, if not first-hand, seems a likely close second-hand. There seems little doubt that Leila would have told Angela all the details of her 'post'.*

They shared everything from their first meeting at the Rusholme tea-party. Angela introduced Leila to one of her favourite books, George Macdonald's *The Princess and the Goblin*, and they built their own goblin palace in the nursery, reaching it by labyrinthine passages and caves made with chairs covered by shawls, table-cloths and rugs. At the end of the tunnel the fire glowed behind its guard. Leila's daughter, Carol, remembers Angela (same house, same nursery) constructing a similar series of corridors and caverns a generation later, and crawling through them with as much excitement as when she and Leila had acted out the stirring adventures in the 80s.

It was at that time that Angela first began writing. She had, from her first reading days, been an admirer of *Little Folks*, published by Cassell and Co., and she now decided that she and Leila must produce their own magazine. They both wrote a serial, Leila's entitled *Fairy Silverstar* and Angela's *Prince Azib*. In each issue there were riddles, acrostics and short stories, one of which (by Angela) always illustrated a moral. Nothing survived but two poems, one a joint effort entitled 'Fairy Frolics', and the other 'The Kitten's Chorus' by Angela alone, which she passed on to the inventive muse of one Sylvia Linsay from *The Third Class at Miss Kaye's* (which was, aptly, her third book).

Sylvia was the founder of the Secret Society of Literary Under-takings, and her verses 'proved so popular' with the other members that it was read aloud many times. 'It was the first time that the class had heard any of Sylvia's effusions and they were quite impressed.'

---

* Angela's own subsequent short period as a governess was kept a guarded secret.

In 1922 a schoolgirl (a real one) wrote to Angela Brazil in appreciation, at the same time informing her that she 'edited' a magazine in aid of the Little Folks' Home in Bexhill. By this time Angela herself had written for *Little Folks*, the magazine she had once emulated, and she answered on pale pink paper.

My dear Elsie,

Thank you for your nice letter. I am glad to hear you and your friends at school like my books. I am very busy writing another just at present.

I am glad you have a magazine in aid of the 'Little Folks'' Home in Bexhill. I have always loved 'Little Folks' and have been interested in the cot! Yes, go on and write poems for it! They are excellent practice! I used to run a manuscript magazine myself when I was ten years old. One of the poems I wrote for it is given on p. 161 of *The Third Class at Miss Kaye's*, 'The Kitten's Chorus'.

I also ran a sketching club at school when I was 15. We used to do paintings every month for it. Such societies are great fun, and really very helpful. I wish your magazine every success.

With my love,
Yours very sincerely,
Angela Brazil.

Perhaps two years afterwards, when she was writing *My Own Schooldays* for the many girl readers 'who have written to ask what I did in my own schooldays', she had Elsie's letter in mind as she set out *The Kitten's Chorus* for the third time.

Miew! Miew! Miew! Miew!
We want to catch mice, we do, we do!
But our mother, the old white cat,
Says we are rather too young for that.

Miew! Miew! Miew! Miew!
We want to catch flies, we do, we do!
But our mother says that if we do it
We'll grow so thin that we soon shall rue it!

Miew! Miew! Miew! Miew!
We want to catch mother's tail we do!

But she says she is not such a common cat
As to let her kits be so pert as that.

Mothers – even mothers of kittens – were aware of the social niceties which Angela continued to pass on to her readers in the line of duty whenever she had the chance.

[5]
HEAD GIRL

Leila was already at Ellerslie when Angela joined the school, and Angelica must have relaxed in the knowledge that school and home were at last in harmony. Her own school, which Angela was to transmute into fiction as The Hollies in *The Fortunes of Philippa*, had been unique. The curriculum had been similar in many ways to that prescribed by Miss Clough for Mary Arnold, but the conditions were kinder – although not much. The high standard of teaching Angelica had enjoyed was now available to Angela, for the classes were small and the work stimulating. Angela did not have to sit straight with a backboard as her mother had done, but the Ellerslie girls *were* drilled weekly by an officer, who taught them to make a graceful bow when passing an acquaintance in the street. The surroundings were congenial: pleasant grounds, polished floors in the classrooms, forms covered in red baize, pictures on the walls. Angelica probably congratulated herself that she had been able to give Angela the best of both worlds, the quiet cultured environment of a first-rate school in conjunction with an encouraging and loving family.

Boarding-school had brought Angelica to the verge of a nervous breakdown, and one cannot help speculating on the content of Angela's literary work had she too been packed off to such a strictly run establishment, far from the sympathies of home. Her penetration of Philippa's (Angelica's) mental state exceeds anything she was to write afterwards. Other heroines, including the early ones, lack consistent psychological accuracy, and I think this had to do not with Angela's but with Angelica's story-telling art. She was a born *raconteuse*, and I am sure that from the Preston days onwards Angela had begged her mother for stories of 'when you were a little girl'. This is not to denigrate Angela's own contribution; it is due to her ability as a writer that the chapter 'A Hard Time' (reproduced here as Appendix A) gives such compassionate insight into adolescent duress, remarkable for its period. It was written in 1905 and it is only surprising that the contemplation of her mother's stress and misery did not put her off boarding-schools for life!

Ellerslie provided no such traumas. At the worst it gave Angela bad dreams of attending class with her work unprepared, dreams which continued into adult life. 'I awake,' she said in 1924, 'with a sense of intense relief that my schooldays are all over!' An astonishing admission!

'My goodness, they educated those girls!' said Leila's daughter. She was right. They were shored-up with literature, a lifetime's reference bank of quotations, a source of continual pleasure.

In every form there were at least three weekly lessons, one on the history of literature, including the lives and main works of all British authors from Anglo-Saxon times to Victorian days, and the rest on selected plays and poems. Chaucer, Spenser, Shakespeare, Milton, Defoe, Pope, Charles Lamb, and many another literary worthy became as household names. We knew every intimate detail of their biographies. We read extracts from their works and criticisms of their style. We learnt the rules of prosody and scanned their poems. We were taught the intricacies of the construction of a sonnet, and knew the difference between epics, lyrics and the rest of it. Certain Shakespeare plays we studied exhaustively with notes, also *Lycidas, Il Penseroso, Marmion, The Lady of the Lake*, Bacon's *Essays*, and other classics. We copied voluminous notes, made by our teacher, on the more modern authors, Keats, Shelley, Tennyson, Browning and Ruskin. We read Dickens aloud.

It would be surprising if some of the knowledge and appreciation had not spilled into the books, and of course it did, but never intrusively. Yet despite the benefits Angela acquired from her formal teaching she was more concerned with amateur arts, that enviable aspect of school life which Ellerslie did not provide. Angela was convinced (ahead of her time) of the benefits of participation and creation. Because she never had the opportunity to act in a school play, there is scarcely a school of her invention in which the dramatics society did not have at least a chapter to itself. In *The School on the Moor*, the girls enjoyed 'Wet Day Dramatics'. In *The Madcap of the School* there was a Coon Concert in aid of the Blinded Soldiers' Fund ('You sing plantation songs, and wear red-and-white costume, and wave tambourines, and that sort of thing'). In *The School on the Cliff* the girls of IVA performed an operetta ('laid in Wales in the olden days of Romance') and Miss Macmillan, head of St Oran's in *The School on the Loch*, took over the Guildhall and put on a Scottish Concert which included Greek dancing and a performance by violin prodigy Sonia Scheffenoska who played the *Liebesfreud* by Kreisler! The details of rehearsals were painstakingly recorded, often for their own sake, but sometimes to illuminate character. The 'Amateur Theatricals' in *A Fourth Form Friendship* showed Aldred in a poor light ('She was very disgusted to be obliged to take such a humble part') but Philippa had her moment of deserved glory, to the chagrin of loathsome Ernestine Salt ('We were called before the curtain at the end of the performance, and the audience broke into ringing cheers for Portia'), and earned the right to become a member of the Dramatics Society. When the boarders performed *Lady Tracy's at Home* in *For the School Colours*, they were up-staged by the day-girls, and found themselves acting to a half-empty house ('The stage of the future is going to be a School of Education for the People,' moralized Adah. 'Conscientious and cultured actresses will never be a want'); the tableaux in the dormitory in *The Feast in No 7** (they included Bluebeard and a reproduction of Millais's *The Black Brunswickers' Departure*) brought out the best in senior Laura Hammond who did not tell tales.

It is significant that Angela had no interest in the professional theatre, yet she could write feelingly that after she had left Ellerslie

> a gymnasium was built and provided with an up-to-date stage, curtain, footlights, greenroom etc., where most splendid theatricals were performed by the pupils with the perfection of dress and scenery . . . *how* I should have enjoyed it . . . Why, school would have been Paradise.

Her outlook on art remained parochial; there is evidence to show that the fruition of talent in fiction and in life (with the

---

* Published in a collected edition of short stories, *Queen of the Dormitory*.

exception of Amy's and her own) ceased to concern her. She wanted only to encourage the young to fulfil themselves artistically, but once they were set on the professional path she did not care. Her books are full of youthful struggles not merely in theatricals, but in singing, painting and music.

Perhaps Angela was thinking of her father and his thwarted talent when Clifford, in *Schoolgirl Kitty*, was told by *his* father: 'I'll send no son of mine to waste time at the School of Art. There's some work to be done in the world. You'll have to put your shoulder to the wheel.' *Schoolgirl Kitty* and *The Head Girl at the Gables* have plots which are closely involved with Art-as-a-Way-of-Life. The beautiful, bohemian and fecund Castleton family were all gifted.

Mr Castleton, absorbed in a classic painting of Beata and Romola as wood nymphs, detached his mind with difficulty from Greek draperies and focussed it upon his eldest daughter. 'I didn't know Claudia could sing!' he remarked with surprise.

In the same book (in which the various members of the family express themselves by playing the organ, singing, sculpting and painting) Margaret Lindsay, an artist, gave a homily on fashions in art to schoolgirl Lorraine which is typical of Angela's method of passing on information and opinions to her readers.

'... people tire of one style and like another. First the classical school was the favourite, then pre-Raphaelitism had its innings, then impressionism came up. Each period in painting is generally boomed by some celebrated art critic who deprecates the old-fashioned methods and cracks up the new. The public are rather like sheep. They buy what the critics tell them to admire. *Punch* had a delightful skit on that once. Ruskin had been pitching into the commonplace artist's style of picture rather freely, so *Punch* evolved a dejected brother of the brush giving vent to this despairing wail:

'I takes and paints,
Hears no complaints,
And sells before I'm dry;
The savage Ruskin
He sticks his tusk in,
And nobody will buy!'

'I love *Punch*!' cackled Lorraine, drying the brushes on a clean paint-rag. 'Tell me some more artistic titbits.'

Angela had always enjoyed drawing and painting. While she was at Ellerslie she began to paint a series of wild flowers, each labelled with a quotation from literature, an idea she had after winning a prize for a school literary competition. (Leila had come second!) She continued with this hobby over many years, and the collection is now in the Herbert Art Gallery in Coventry, although not on show.

After she left Manchester High School, Amy studied at the School of Art, joining a sketching club in her free time. Angela often posed for her, and had dreams of following her in her career. The whole family were inspired by the ambience; Walter, in his limited spare time, sketched rare flowers, archaeological finds and architecture; Clarence (senior) began to draw again, which he had not done for years, and even Angelica, whose talents were literary rather than visual, brought out her pencils and sketch-book.

Angela and Amy began to look beyond Manchester to Paris, the artist's Mecca. Like Lesbia Ferrars in *Loyal to the School* they must have thought that 'a course at a Paris studio was as impossible as a tour round the world'. Art student Clifford achieved the dream, together with his sister Kitty. ('Isn't it wonderful and glorious just to be alive – in Paris?' she said.) *Schoolgirl Kitty*, written in 1924, long after Amy and Angela's student aspirations – they did *not* then study in Paris, although Amy did later – is an important book to which I will return later; a key work, not only because of its content, but because of people and events which initiated it.

Angela Brazil created her own image. ('You only knew,' said a friend, 'what she wanted you to know.') Her autobiography was a very careful and contrived account, and one of the affectations she thought to impress upon her schoolgirl readers was her musicality. Angela was never musical, as those who heard her sing *Somewhere a Voice is Calling* to Amy's piano accompaniment have testified. Amy and Walter were the able instrumentalists, and, I am inclined to believe, the ones with the genuine knowledge and appreciation. Angela did buy a guitar on her travels,* and Carol (Leila's daughter) remembers that one night, when she and her sister Mary were in bed, an awful noise arose, which made Mary cry with fear.

* She would play it wearing Spanish dress and shawl, finishing with a sweep of her hand in the grand manner. She called it her mandolin.

When she was told that it was 'Auntie Angela's mandolin', she thought it was Auntie Angela mangling, an explanation which satisfied her completely, and became a family joke that was never divulged to Angela, who would not have been amused.

Music, nevertheless, has a central function in a number of the novels, and for those heroines it was a focal point of their lives, with Mildred Lancaster of St Cyprian's the prime exponent.

The Girls of St Cyprian's came out in 1914, and Angela received among her growing fan mail two letters concerning its origins.

Dear Madam,

I have just completed perusal of your very interesting and clever book, *The Girls of St Cyprian's*, and myself a Manchester woman by birth and early associations I venture to ask if you will tell me whether Kirkton stands for Manchester as I think it very well might, and going a step further whether St Cyprian's is Ellerslie in Victoria Park?

The second letter (more personal) came from a schoolteacher. She said:

One of my girls recently came to me saying that she had been reading a new book which her aunt had given her. She was charmed with it. It was 'ripping' as she phrased it. On looking to see what manner of book this might be, behold it was a school tale by Angela Brazil. 'Angela Brazil' I gasped. 'Surely there couldn't be two Angela Brazils, this must be our Angela.' Thereupon I borrowed the work and took it home to read and discovered signs of Ellerslie running all through it.

Since Ellerslie had no extra-mural activities or sports, and since in the very first chapter Miss Cartwright formed an alliance with five other schools competing in Music, Drama, Arts, Handicrafts, Literature and Games, there must be other internal evidence to distinguish it. The most likely source is the music curriculum, and that Kirkton, too, is identifiable by its musical reputation. (*I* thought I recognized signs of Coventry, where Angela was living when she wrote the book; the Kirkton Herald is in Corporation Street where the Coventry newspaper offices are.)

Manchester was, arguably, then as now, the most musical city in England, with the obvious exception of London. When Angela was at school her sister and brothers, whenever they were able, went to the Hallé concerts; both Clarence and Walter played in the university orchestra, and had musically gifted friends. One in particular

> could play ten different instruments . . . and who might have made a great name for himself, but, alas! when skating at Geneva, he ventured on thin ice, and the dark waters of the lake wiped out his future career.

Amy was studying the piano under the tuition of one of the many German teachers in the city and 'we talked constantly of Beethoven, Mozart, Wagner, Handel, Berlioz', boasted Angela. She had once taken lessons from Amy's teacher, but he despaired of her ability and the subject was dropped until she suddenly decided, at Ellerslie, that she wanted to learn at school. By her own account she did rather well. Continuing the self-delusion she said: 'It is a coincidence that years afterwards I was told in my horoscope that music had been for me a rather neglected talent.'

Musical talents were not neglected at Ellerslie. They were the *raison d'être* of the only quasi-social function of the school year – the concert followed by the prize-giving. On one of these occasions Angela actually sang a solo; she was the favourite pupil of the Bavarian singing mistress who composed many of the simple songs she taught the girls. Her songs and her accent were mimicked by everyone, but Angela rather liked her. She said that in retrospect she put this Fraulein in a mental compartment with some little Nuremberg toys she bought at the Christmas German Fair in Manchester, a patronizing assessment but not a surprising one to any reader of Angela's work, where foreigners (except of course *girl* foreigners) were either evil or comic. The singing mistress was very particular about the position of the mouth and she saw Angela as its perfect exponent, frequently inviting her to the front of the class to demonstrate, which was both hilarious and embarrassing. She did not appear in *The Girls of St Cyprian's*, but her manner of speech was transferred to the violin teacher Herr Hoffmann (and to many another German member of staff elsewhere) who organized the students' concerts in Kirkton.

> 'Unsinn!' (which is German for 'stuff and nonsense') cried the Professor. 'You will do what I say. You shall work at ze "Fruhlingslied", and each Sunday afternoon you shall come to rehearse it with my students' orchestra at ze Philharmonic Hall. Yes, I have said it!'

Mildred, who had inherited talent and a Stradivarius from her father, turned aside a future in the lap of landed aristocracy for her art. It says much for Angela that in her presentation of the philistine Sir Darcy and Lady Lorraine, she did not condemn their way of life, but gave a fair and often attractive account of it, thus making Mildred's choice genuinely difficult.

Miss Cartwright, principal of St Cyprian's, was a more accessible figure than Ellerslie's Miss Millington. Once, when Angela's family suggested that she should borrow a book from the headmistress (she needed to draw a sloth for a geography lesson), Angela received the idea with derision.

> Ask Miss Millington? I would as soon have journeyed to Buckingham Palace and borrowed a book from the Queen! The library was a sacred temple of our headmistress, into which we were ushered to report ourselves if we lost conduct marks! I would not knock at its portals unless compelled!

(Gipsy Latimer made the mistake of broaching Miss Poppleton's study in *The Leader of the Lower School*.)

Angela was keenly conscious of the responsibilities of headmistresses, and her books embrace a comprehensive range from the kind, understanding and sporting Miss Suffolk of *The Little Green School* – 'Away went Miss Suffolk with (butterfly) net, plunging courageously through nettles and brambles in chase of her elusive quarry' – to stern Miss Farrar of St Monica's, whose dominating presence loomed menacingly throughout 'The Tradition of the School', a short story in *Bosom Friends*.

> She was treated at St Monica's with the respect yielded to the abbess of a convent or the president of a republic.
> 'If you happen to meet Miss Farrar in one of the passages,' explained Mab to Meta, 'you've got to walk along two steps behind her for a little way, just *in case* she might wish to speak to you.'

(This is not as far-fetched as it might seem when one remembers that the real girls of Harrogate College in the 1940s began term with a ceremonial parade before their principal, names round their necks, each bowing to her as they passed.)

In greater or lesser ways, however, from the stern to the sympathetic, Angela's headmistresses all instilled awe, obedience and admiration.

Angela Brazil aged sixty

Above left Child portrait of Angela by Amy Brazil

Below left Illustration used for *A Terrible Tomboy*: Peggy by Amy and Angela Brazil

Above right Drawing of Leila in plum coloured pinafore by Angela Brazil aged te[n]

Below right A botanical drawing by Angel[a] Brazil in her last year of school

Above Angelica Brazil in her cottage in Wales

Below Ffynnonbedr, the Brazil's cottage in Llanbedr

Above The Quadrant, Coventry (extreme right) Angela's home from 1911 and inset, Angela aged forty

Above right Angela visiting Arley Castle School in 1928

Below right Angela Brazil (centre) and members of the Coventry City Guild in 1922

Amy Brazil

Walter Brazil M.D.

Above Picnic at Watergate (Angela and Walter standing, Amy seated right) 17 August 1922

Below Angela Brazil's cottage, The Haven, in Polperro, Cornwall, as it is today (white semi-detached, centre)

Avelyn and the Lavender Lady
and inset, the Lavender Lady's
prototype, Angela Brazil

THE FORTUNES
OF PHILIPPA
ANGELA BRAZIL

THE FORTUNES
of PHILIPPA
Angela Brazil

THE FORTUNES
OF PHILIPPA
ANGELA BRAZIL

Patriotic schoolgirls
1918 and 1941

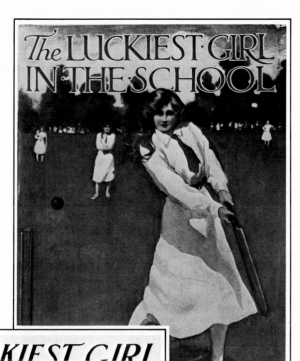

The Luckiest Girl in the School. Winona Woodward on both sides of the Atlantic

FERN SEED.

THE NEW WORLD MUSIC PUB: CO. SMETHWICK

'I'm bored stiff,' confessed Delia in *The School in the South*. 'Renie, if you love me, take me out of earshot of Miss Morley and let me chatter and frivol.'

And in *The School on the Moor*, Miss Lindon B.A. ordered:

'I shall blow my whistle twice when it is time to return, then each teacher will also blow her whistle, and every girl must at once come back to the beach, where I shall take the register before we start back, to make sure that nobody is missing.'

Miss Lindon was both 'athletic and intellectual'; Miss Drummond, in *A Fourth Form Friendship*, 'had the rare quality of absolute tact and sympathy', and what is more she allowed her pupils hot bricks in bed on cold nights, a privilege denied to Angela when her feet froze in the Ellerslie hostel during her last winter at the school. Mrs Morris also permitted hot bricks for cold toes in *A Patriotic Schoolgirl*, but like most of her colleagues she was adamant on matters of honour.

'Girls who have deliberately broken rules, defied the authority of my colleague, which is equivalent to defying me, and have lowered the prestige of the school in the eyes of the world, deserve the contempt of their comrades, who, I hope, will show their opinion of such conduct.'

Not surprisingly her diatribe, directed at poor Margery Anderson, reduced the girl to tears.

The common situation of sisters-in-authority provided much material for Angela, who had had first-hand experience of the Misses Knowles and the Misses Allison, and knew of at least three sets in Coventry when she was actively writing. Miss Poppleton's hauteur (she was a *double* B.A.) in *The Leader of the Lower School* was offset by kind Miss Edith ('if Miss Poppleton's scolding had been hard to endure, Miss Edith's concern was far worse'). My own favourites, I think, are the principals of Aireyholme, in *The Jolliest Term on Record*.

Tall, massive, perhaps even a trifle masculine in appearance, Mrs Franklin hid a really kind heart under a rather uncompromising and masterful manner. She was a clever manager, an admirable housekeeper, and ruled her little kingdom both well and wisely. Both in features and personality she resembled an ancient Roman matron, and among the girls she was often known as 'the mother of Gracchi'. Mrs Franklin's sister, Miss Aubrey, who lived at the school, was an artist of considerable talent.

The girls, under their liberal and artistic regime, were remarkably free from stress, as were the pupils of that gentle and unabrasive pair Miss Pollard and Miss Fanny of Devonshire in *A Fortunate Term.*

'They're dears, both of them,' thought Mavis. 'Absolute dears! Anybody more unlike schoolmistresses I have never met in my life. They ought to have been married. They must have been so pretty when they were young. I suppose they never met anybody in this out-of-the-way place. The school may be old-fashioned, and behind the age, and all the rest of it, but they give the boarders a good time at any rate. They're just mothers to those Indian children. I'm glad to have had a peep behind the scenes and seen this side of them. I believe I'm rather in love with them both.'

Sometimes Angela contrasted the two extreme types of principal in one book. The unenlightened and unlovable Miss Selwyn in *Ruth of St Ronan's*, who considered half-term holidays disruptive and did all she could to prevent parents from taking out their daughters, was counterbalanced by Miss Turrell ('tall and athletic, and rather masculine in appearance, with a deep commanding voice') who ran the winter sports holiday. In *The Little Green School*, problems of the future were solved when Miss Suffolk decided to share her headship with Miss Horace. ('Miss Horace is more up to date and gives us games,' ventured Enid. 'Aunt Selina says Miss Horace gives us "education" and Miss Suffolk gives us "culture",' said Betty.)

Possibly Angela felt that the embodiment of all the ideal qualities was too much for one woman. Miss Kingsley and Miss Janet (sisters again) made an admirable job of running The Gables in artistic Porthkeverne in Cornwall, teaching the children of 'painters and authors, though a few of the gentry and professional men of the district also took advantage of such good local opportunity to educate their daughters'. The cultured atmosphere was perfectly portrayed in the opening chapter 'A Momentous

Decision', as the principals debate on who should be *The Head Girl at the Gables*.

It was exactly ten days before the opening of the autumn term at The Gables. The September sunshine, flooding through the window of the Principal's study, lighted up the bowl of carnations upon the writing table, and flashed back from the Chippendale mirror on the wall, caught the book-case with the morocco-bound editions of the poets, showed up the etching of 'Dante's Dream' over the mantelpiece, and glowed on Miss Kingsley's ripply brown hair, turning all the silver threads to gold. Miss Kingsley, rested and refreshed after the long summer holiday, a touch of pink in her cheeks and a brightness in her eyes, left as a legacy from the breezes of the Cheviot Hills, was seated at her desk with a notebook in front of her and a fountain pen in her hand, making plans for a fresh year's work.

Miss Janet, armed with a stump of pencil and the back of an envelope, ready to jot down suggestions, swayed to and fro in the rocking-chair with her lips drawn into a bunch and the particular little pucker between her eyebrows that always came when she was trying to concentrate her thoughts.

'It really *is* a difficulty, Janet!' said Miss Kingsley. 'A suitable head girl makes all the difference to a school, and if we happen to choose the wrong one it may completely spoil the tone.'

Such a momentous choice (Lorraine, an 'outsider', needless to say turned out tops) was never faced by Miss Millington at Ellerslie. Her head girls, and Angela was one of them, were selected solely by virtue of work. Angela bemoaned the fact that it

was an empty title that carried no authority beyond the mere honour of it. How I should have adored the privileges of the modern head girl! The small children always attracted me, and it would have been a labour of love to organise their games or train them to act a fairy play. As it was, I fancy a certain amount of my energy ran to waste.

The energy that was conserved went into creating head girls and prefects that have already pleased at least five generations (with more to come). They were a motley assembly who faced the tasks denied to the girls of Ellerslie. Angela believed absolutely that a structure of the kind employed by the boys' public schools, with a hierarchy that devolved through the school itself, was far superior to the two-tier teachers-and-girls system she had known. Prefects gained essential knowledge of citizenship and social service, and she put forward her views by the age-old method of attacking the concept first.

'Have you heard the news?' exploded Kitty Harden, tramping noisily into the Fourth Form room one Wednesday morning and banging down her dispatch-box with such energy the corner burst. 'We're actually going to have prefects!'

'Of course we've heard, you old bluebottle!' grunted Alice Drummond rather sulkily. 'You needn't look as if you thought you were giving us a surprise. Why it's all over the school by this time!'

'Quite a chestnut!' yawned Monica Ward.

'I knew about it last night from Betty,' chirruped Marie Parks. 'Miss Boddington told the Sixth yesterday.'

'Well, I've only just heard,' retorted Kitty, 'and I must say it gives me spasms. What in the name of all creation is Miss Boddington thinking about?'

'That's what we're all asking,' interposed the injured voice of Hilda Johnstone. 'If she'd done it when we opened in September or had waited till after Christmas it would have seemed more decent . . . Well, I call it a grizzly swindle!'

'Who wants prefects?' groaned Elizabeth Holmes. 'The school's done very well without them for all these years, and I can't see why they should be fastened on us now!'

The story, *The Fourth Form Strike*, ended, naturally, with a vote of confidence in the new system, both prefects and fourth formers gaining by it and discovering that the school itself was a microcosm. 'A large school', Angela wrote in *The Leader of the Lower School*,

is a state in miniature. Quite apart from the rule of the mistresses, it has its own particular institutions and its own system of self-government. In their special domain its officers are of quite as much importance as Members of Parliament, comparable to that of Cabinet Ministers. Tyrannies, struggles for freedom, minor corruptions, and hot debates have their places here as well as in the wider world of politics, and many an amateur 'Home Rule Bill' is defeated or carried according to the circumstances of the case.

The revolutionary programme that Gipsy Latimer introduced to Briarcroft Hall, smashing the existing oligarchy, running an effective *Juniors' Journal* (at one point she was accused of failing to maintain it as a representative organ) and yet retaining the essential loyalty to her *alma mater*, expounds the core of Angela's creed. It is a surprisingly contemporary exposé of pupil-power. Written in late 1912 it was an astonishing achievement.

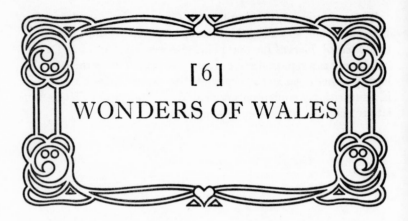

[6]
WONDERS OF WALES

The Brazils made their final family move in 1887, to 4 High View, Belmont, on the edge of Bolton moors. Presumably the departure from Manchester was caused by the demands of the cotton trade, because they viewed it with reluctance and displeasure.

'Bolton,' said Angela, 'was a penance to artistic minds.'

The narrow streets and belching factory chimneys were anathema to them all. The sole compensation was that the new house was outside the town limits, and was 'very old and quaint and had a glorious garden'. The cat, Desdemona, preferred it to the one she had left behind.

The main problem which faced Angelica was Angela's schooling. The prospect of finding a day-school in Bolton which was comparable to Ellerslie was so improbable that it was decided she should complete her education in Manchester, boarding in one of the hostels connected with the school.

'We had all sorts of dormitory fun,' Angela recalled, and needless to say it found its way into the revels of her girls.

    1 box of sardines
    1 currant loaf
    13 oranges
    13 cheese cakes
    $\frac{1}{2}$ lb. Pat-A-Cake biscuits
    Sweets with any money that is left

ran the list for one midnight feast. Japes, jokes and jollities too numerous to catalogue brightened the night lives of the dormitory inhabitants, bringing tense moments of near discovery, revenge and reward. Feigned sleepwalking, mysterious ghosts and the meetings of secret societies gave zest to the hours of darkness.

'I had a terrible fright!' said Nancy Hall. 'Evelyn had gone to bed in such a hurry that she left her foot sticking out from under the clothes, and I was so dreadfully afraid Miss Miller would see it and ask why she hadn't taken her shoes and stockings off. But luckily she didn't.'

'Laura Hammond came upstairs to fetch a clean pocket handkerchief, just when I had put on my nightdress,' said Lottie Greenwood. 'I thought she stared at me very hard, and I certainly must have looked queer and fat, with all my clothes underneath. I wonder if she guesses?'

'I hope Miss Miller doesn't suspect anything,' said Phyllis. 'I think we ought to have a scout at the end of the passage. We can take it in turns. Let us count out who shall go first.'

The others agreed as to the necessary precaution, and the lot fell on Ada Southwell, who departed unwillingly with half a cheese cake to console her, while the rest of the guests seated themselves on Mabel's and Dorothy's beds, and partook of refreshments with much appreciation, particularly enjoying the sips of fizzy lemon kali, hastily mixed in a glass, and stirred with a lead pencil.

Cheesecake must have been a favourite of Angela's since it was the mainstay of feasts! 'If anyone's spirits flagged, the rest had only to whisper "oranges" or "cheesecakes" to restore a smile,' she wrote in 1914 in a short story, 'A Midnight Revel'. In *My Own Schooldays* she reminisced ecstatically over the crumbs in her bed, uncomfortable remnants of the cheesecakes smuggled into the Ellerslie hostel, and washed down with that same lemon kali served in 'our bedroom tumblers'. (Was there no experience that disappeared into Angela's subconscious? Did everything surface for the sake of the schools?)

The hostel routine was tight and somewhat arduous. Angela rose at seven and practised the piano before breakfast and prayers. From nine until twelve-thirty or one o'clock she was in the school building, back at the hostel for lunch and in school again until four. After the hostel tea, she did her preparation and practised the piano until supper at eight. There could not have been much energy left for 'dormitory fun' – or indeed for any kind of amusement during that last year at Ellerslie when the prospect of the approaching Higher School Certificate dominated her life. Like Winona Woodward in *The Luckiest Girl in the School*, 'she often groaned when she thought of the "matric"'. 'Most of our best fun at school happens in our early teens,' she reflected in *Joan's Best Chum*.

'Under twelve' we are apt to have too few privileges, and 'over fifteen' we are generally the victims of preparation for some horrible public examination, and spend all our spare time 'swotting at maths', or committing elusive facts to memory. But those magic years of 'thirteen' and 'fourteen' are a sort of high-water mark, when we have our fling undisturbed by too many restrictions or responsibilities. We have been long enough at school to be entirely in the swim of things, but we are certainly not leaving next term, and need not trouble our heads as yet about future careers.

Frantic cramming with no satisfaction in the work for its own sake spoiled the remaining year of school, and Angela, who regenerated her schooldays from middle to old age, felt an overwhelming relief when the real thing drew to a close and she was free to follow her own pursuits. Whether or not her aspirations included marriage there is nothing to tell us. She was extremely attractive. Her eyes were beautiful. Surely there were suitors? She did not keep a diary, or at least none remains, although she encouraged others to keep records, saying 'they were beyond price' for the recollection of particular events. There are no contemporaries left to gossip, but just occasionally there are hints that not all her hopes were fulfilled. It seems likely that at some time or other (even if not for long) she and Amy must have cherished dreams of romantic matrimony. Perhaps their intellectual demands and the family clannishness were intimidating.

It is few of us who are able to realize all the glorious castles in the air we plan when we are young; and fate, who decrees what is best for us, often urges our footsteps along unknown paths.

Many people have remarked on Angela's shyness, so perhaps she was speaking for herself when Loveday (in *A Harum Scarum Schoolgirl*), 'plying her hairbrush, shook her long flaxen mane dolefully' and replied to Diana's question, 'But aren't you going to get married?' with considered conclusions.

'I don't say I wouldn't *like* to. But I don't think it's at all likely. I'm not an attractive kind of girl; I know that well enough. I'm so shy. I never know what to say to people when they begin to talk to me. They must think me a silly goose . . . I don't suppose anybody'll ever trouble to look at me twice.'

Incipient romances do occur in the first batch of books from Angela's pen; there is the token love interest between Daphne and Captain Harper in *For the School Colours* (although the real love story is not theirs), and in *Monitress Merle* is the hint that in years to come Mavis might become Bevis's wife. Appropriately that chapter is called 'Love in the Mist!' Marjorie Anderson's sad reflections on Lieutenant Preston and the 'certain chapter of her life, which had seemed to promise many very sweet hopes and was now forever closed' proved to be unfounded, for in *The School in the South* (they first met in *A Patriotic Schoolgirl*) they turn up on Capri, where Peachy whispered to Irene one evening: 'I do believe those two are "a case",' and Irene answered:

'So do I. They first met when Marjorie was at school. Dona told me all about¹ it, and it was quite romantic. They'd have seen more of each other, only, after the armistice, his regiment was ordered out to India.'

Marriages (with the exception of Lilian's to the Rector of Gorswen in the retrospective round-up at the end of *A Terrible Tomboy*) were strictly for adults. Aunt Helen, who made a late attachment, advised Peggy:

'If you quarrel with anyone, go and fight it out at once, and get it over, and don't let misunderstandings make the breach so wide that nothing can ever mend it again.'

Was Angela thinking back to some episode in her own youth, or in Amy's? She was thirty-five when she wrote *A Terrible Tomboy*, and spinsterhood was by then almost a certainty. The only possible prospects were lonely widowers – and for a short time, so rumour has it, Angela had one in mind – like the bereaved and musical Dr Linton who married dark-eyed, clever but sarcastic Miss Strong, form mistress of VA at Grovebury College in *A Popular Schoolgirl*.

'Hold me up!' she murmured dramatically. 'Why, I didn't know he was a widower!'

'Of course he is,' endorsed Ingrid, 'and a most uncomfortable one, I should say. I went to his house once for a music lesson, and it looked in a fearful muddle. Good old Bantam! We must give her congrats! She'll soon get things into order there! I believe she adores little Kenneth. I've often seen her taking him about the town. She shall have my blessing, by all means!'

Even boys – and they have a function somewhere down the scale from secret societies and dormitory feasts – do not stir the girlish breasts. With only a few half-hearted exceptions they remain brothers. Winona Woodward, for one, kept a

... special album in which she posted photos of him in khaki, all his letters and postcards, and any newspaper cuttings that concerned his regiment. The book was already half full; she looked it over almost daily, and kept it as, at present, her greatest treasure.

She sent parcels regularly to Percy. Campaigning had not destroyed his boyish love for sweetstuff, and he welcomed cakes, toffee and chocolate. 'I share it with the other chaps,' he wrote, 'and they give you a vote of thanks every time. You wouldn't believe what larks we have in our dug-out!'

How much jollier to have a brother larking in a dug-out than a sweetheart mooning over the girl he left behind. Walter, too old to take part in the First World War, was the outstanding male influence in Angela's life; Jim Stanfield, in *The School on the Moor*, received Angela's highest accolade. Not only was he 'an outstanding character, a most attractive boy and an immense addition to the party' but she cleverly removed him from the dangerous zone of friendship (where he began) to become – what else? – a step-brother. Such a relief for Brenda! She gained a brother and a mother. Who would want more than that?

It wasn't only Marjorie Anderson who transmigrated from one novel to another. Angela had a number of itinerant characters, including Peachy and Irene (who met Marjorie on Capri on her second published appearance) on holiday at Menton in *Joan's Best Chum*. More complex was the arrival of the new English teacher at The Moorings in *A Fortunate Term* who had been educated at St Cyprian's College and whose girlish exploits were familiar to Angela's readers. Now on the side of authority, all the precepts she had been taught at her *alma mater* benefited Mavis and Merle, whose mother's cousin Sheila was a friend of Miss Mitchell's. Sheila? Mitchell? Of course! Eve Mitchell and Sheila More, grown-up, still corresponding, and what a comfort to know they remained in their academic orbit, teaching, organizing clubs for schoolgirls and writing news to one another. Eve Mitchell, whose function was limited in her schooldays at St Cyprian's, grew to be of supreme importance to the development of her girls in *Monitress Merle*.

Soon after leaving Ellerslie, Angela went with Amy to London to attend Heatherley's art school. It has not been possible to ascertain the actual dates since Heatherley's moved in 1969 and all the old records were thrown away. This has been a repetitive situation and a constant source of frustration in my search for the documentation of the Brazils. Amy, at some time during the period between Heatherley's and the move to Coventry, trained as a nurse at Queen Charlotte's Hospital in London. Queen Charlotte's register does not go back that far. Walter's history is likewise unrecorded both at Barts, where he was a student, and at the hospital in Warwickshire where he held a post until 1946. Clarence's legal studies have been impossible to place or date. Even more surprising is that Blackie's, Angela's publishers for forty years, should have retained no correspondence. Nelson's, who also published her, have nothing but a catalogue. The bombing of Coventry destroyed files which would have enabled me to dispense with speculation, but the greatest loss was an incomplete manuscript and twenty years of personal letters thrown away only months before I advertised for material. It is, nevertheless, safe to assume that Angela was between seventeen and nineteen when she left Bolton temporarily for London and a course in art.

Katrine looked artistic to her fingertips. She was just seventeen, and, owing to her extreme predilection for painting, had persuaded her parents to take her from the High School, and let her attend the School of Art, where she could devote all her energies to her pet subject.

Katrine (in *The Jolliest Term on Record*) is closer to Amy than Angela, but by the time Amy was enrolled at Heatherley's she had to be in her twenties, and, since she was chaperoning her younger sister, presumably over twenty-one. It seems highly probable that during this period Walter was also in London, and that the three younger Brazils lived together as they were to do again later. If there had been a repeat of 'hostel-fun' there is no doubt that

Angela would have said so. It is most likely that they stayed at the Kenilworth (then a temperance hotel) close to the British Museum, which they used subsequently whenever they came to London. ('We *always* stay at the Ken-il-worth,' Angela would say in her carefully modulated manner to Coventry acquaintances.) Heatherley's was on the verge of Bloomsbury, being then in Newman Street in the triangle between Oxford Street and the Tottenham Court Road, and within comfortable walking distance of the hotel.

The school had an illustrious roll of past students, which included Millais, Rossetti and Burne-Jones. Angela described the studios where she worked, an outer room where she 'drew from the antique' and 'an inner sanctum where the costume model posed daily from 10 till 4 o'clock'. The school was famed, she said, for its *tableaux vivants*, with the models dressed elaborately as Arab Sheiks or Spanish maidens from Old Seville. Painters who were not full-time students made use of the facilities, and Angela noted conversations she had had at the easel with Sir Henry Irving's understudy and the Baroness Orczy, an unexpected pair!

The Brazil family had always been keen museum-goers. Angela had been taken to Brown's Museum in Liverpool when she was seven, which had first excited her interest in Egyptology. In *St Catherine's College* Miss Kirk became quite exhausted as she escorted a selected party from IVA around the British Museum. There is a detailed description of the exhibits in Room 111, and Angela, who had what amounted to an obsession with hair (she constantly exclaimed over its loveliness in fiction and life) extended the fascination to the mummified Kleopatra of Thebes.

'Only eleven! She was younger than we are!' said Rachel.

'I dare say she was pretty,' said Beryl, examining the portrait carefully. (It was on the mummy-cloth.) 'You can see she had lovely wide-open dark eyes and a beautiful mouth, and plenty of brown curly hair.'

'Was that the comb she used for it?' asked Allie. 'Would she be dark or fair?'

Angela, in the company of her fellow students, went frequently to museums and galleries, the British Museum and the Royal Academy being the top two on her list. She said: 'It is wonderful to be young in the midst of a circle of aspiring friends,' but there is no indication that the friends remained in her circle; indeed, it is probable that they did not. I doubt whether the Heatherley's period was very long. More important and of lasting influence were the sketching holidays which she took with Amy over a number of summers, in Warwickshire, Herefordshire, the Lake District, and most important of all, in Wales.

Wales was central to Angela's life and work. Not only the mountainous landscape but Celtic mythology gave her intense pleasure and mental sustenance that verged on the numinous. Without it her books would have been very different.

The Brazils came to Wales through Amy. There was an artist's society of a kind, and her sketching club arranged a holiday in Llanbedr, overlooking the Conway Valley. Amy was enamoured, and so were her brothers who joined her there. When a cottage became empty she suggested to her parents that they should take it, and, enterprising people that they were, Clarence and Angelica agreed. 'In these modern days,' Angela wrote in 1924, 'country cottages are the fashion, and more in favour than seaside lodgings, but in my early teens it was considered a most unconventional idea, almost like announcing that one was going to spend one's holidays in a pig-stye.'

Angela, who was fourteen, found in Llanbedr the sense of freedom she had once enjoyed at Egremont. 'In Manchester,' she said, 'quite against our instincts, we were caged town birds.' From this time on she saw to it that she was never without access to rural life.

Not long after the Brazils acquired their cottage – and it was extremely simple, almost primitive – Leila's parents followed suit, and so fundamental did it become to her, too, that not only her children, but her grandchildren and great-grandchildren grew (and are growing up) with memories of Llanbedr.

To reach it was an adventure. We arrived by train at Tal y Cafn, a wayside station, and were ferried across the River Conway on a broad flat-bottomed boat, worked by chains, sometimes in company with a flock of sheep, or a horse and cart.

The wild countryside gave Angela the feeling that she was close to Nature's heart. She drew water from 'the loveliest "fairy" well on earth, hung over by ferns, and shaded by wild flowers, where the bubbling up of the clear spring took one back to naiads of Ancient Greece or nixies of Celtic legend'.

She gathered sticks for the fire, blackberries for jam and *claimed* to have cleaned a freshly caught trout. She was inspired to write and paint. Her first 'serious' water-colour was a derelict cottage in Llanbedr; her first printed work 'Our Cottage' in the newly started Ellerslie magazine. She liked to think of her existence in Wales as 'half-gipsy'; as a late middle-aged lady she told a friend she was descended from gipsies. I suppose one can give her the benefit of the doubt in some Spanish forbears, but as always with Angela it is difficult to disengage the actual from the image.

She described herself in Llanbedr riding the rector's cob. 'It was pure joy to be on her back,' she said, 'and when she broke into a canter I felt a thorough Diana Vernon' (she meant Dorothy, of course). She was no animal-lover and certainly no rider. What she liked was the concept of herself trotting free along the lanes and across the fields of the Conway Valley. Genuinely rooted in fact, however, were the lessons gained in domesticity. Angelica, who had been brought up to be waited on and then jettisoned to the rigours of an English boarding-school, felt that the cottage was an opportunity to instil her daughters with the arts of housewifery, which she had learned only by trial and error when she married. The mistakes made by Amy and Angela were to be integrated into *A Terrible Tomboy*, and especially into *A Fourth Form Friendship*, where the girls of The Grange learned to prepare meals in a model cottage in the grounds. The blackberry jam that Angela once burned became the disastrous climax to Aldred's attempts at entertaining Miss Drummond.

'There's a queer smell from somewhere!' exclaimed Mabel, who was at the table concocting potato cakes. 'Is anything burning?'

'It's surely not my precious scones!' shrieked Dora, flying to the oven in hot haste, to ascertain the fate of the delicacies in question.

'Why, you only put them in a moment ago!'

'No, it's not the scones; they've hardly begun to cook yet,' said Dora, much relieved. 'Aldred, I believe it's your sugar. Why don't you stir it?'

'I am stirring,' returned Aldred, who, indeed, was wielding the spoon with frantic zeal.

'What's wrong then? Let me try.'

Aldred resigned her weapon, and Dora took her place at the

stove; but she was already too late, for the sugar was rapidly turning into a black solid mass.

'Lift off the pan!' cried Mabel. 'Can't you see it's burning horribly? Oh, what a nasty, disgusting, sticky mess!'

'I don't know why it should have burnt,' complained Aldred. 'I was watching it the whole time.'

'Did you put enough water into it?'

'Water! I didn't put any in at all,' faltered Aldred.

Many incidents, anecdotes and impressions stem from the summers that Angela spent in North Wales during her teens and, indeed, afterwards, for the family continued its association with Llanbedr until 1928. 'It was delightfully free and unconventional', she wrote in *Loyal to the School* of an introductory holiday in Wales,

> almost like camping or caravanning. The younger children ran about without shoes or stockings, nobody wore hats, and gloves were not necessary, even on Sundays . . . her new surroundings were an absolute Paradise. She had, of course, brought her cherished painting materials, and she set to work with wild enthusiasm to try her hand at sketching from nature.

> Even more beautiful perhaps were the bare boughs of the hazel copse, the exquisite tender shades of which were such a subtle blending of purples and greys as to defy the most cunning brush that artist ever wielded, and, contrasted with an occasional pine, or holly, or ivy tree, made a dream of delicate colour. (*For the School Colours.*)

Descriptions of the countryside, and Angela produced many, always failed to produce that ultimate picture for the inner eye, because she could not resist introducing elements of 'faerie' or veering from the visual matter into the nebulous regions of romance, dissipating any effect she had managed to build. Her forte was her girls; she could transmit their 'feelings' for each other but not their feelings for nature. Whimsy intruded, and while it had a distinct charm in the relationships it destroyed the scenery.

Characters, too, had their prototypes in the people she met in the Conway Valley, just as later she found them in Cornwall. The Castletons (from *Monitress Merle* and *The Head Girl at the Gables*) were based on a family which must surely have been the Augustus

Johns. 'With their reputation for beauty, their unusual names, and picturesque garments . . . they always aroused my deepest interest and admiration,' said Angela.

Lorraine's first impression of the Castletons was that they went in for both quality and quantity. They numbered nine, and all had the same nicely-shaped noses, Cupid mouths, irreproachable complexions, neat teeth, dark-fringed blue eyes, and shining sunlit hair. They were a veritable goldmine to artists, and their portraits had been painted constantly by their father and his friends. Pictures of them in various costumes and poses had appeared in coloured supplements to annuals or as frontispieces in magazines; they had figured in the Academy and had been bought for permanent collections in local art galleries. The features of Morland, Claudia, Landry, Beata, Romola and Madox had for years been familiar to frequenters of provincial exhibitions, and sometimes with their lovely mother, whose profile was considered a near approach to the classic statue of Greece.

The lovely mother 'had suddenly resigned all the sad and glad things that make up this puzzle we call life' (one son, the defective one, also crossed the 'divide'), and after mourning for six months, the bereaved husband 'married his model, a girl of barely seventeen, with a beautiful Burne-Jones face and a Cockney accent'. Angela's passion for unusual names had full scope when she granted this new union four more 'carnation cheeked' infants in Constable, Lileth, Perugia and Gabriel (Constable, at seven, 'was generally dressed in a Kate Greenaway smock and his crop of golden hair was still uncut').

With her strong interest in history and mythology, Angela responded with predictable fervour to the Celtic legends and superstitions. She was constantly aware of elements of the ancient past around her, she 'felt as if she held Nature, or something bigger than Nature, tight by the hand'.* The secular and religious music she heard played in the mountain church dated back to before the Saxon psalter. The Minister had the power of the *Hwl*, declaiming his utterances 'on four or five notes, much as his ancestors, the bards, must have poured forth their descriptions of mighty deeds, before chieftains and tribesmen'. The local funerals, dramatic and ritualistic, stirred her deepest emotions.

* *For the School Colours.*

I think Welsh singing in its perfection is heard at a mountain funeral, when the black-clad train of mourners wind slowly across the moor, and down the miles of steep hillside, crooning Celtic laments that might have dropped out of the Bronze Age; the words, indeed, are Christian, yet the swing of the old tunes is prehistoric in the rise and fall of its mystic melancholy.

These experiences fed her susceptibilities and were paralleled by her growing idea of herself. She was writing about Angela Brazil and not Lesbia Ferrars when she described her heroine in *Loyal to the School.*

Lesbia, at fifteen and three-quarters on the great clock of life, [one hopes it was not a 24-hour clock] was a rather picturesque little person, slim and not over-tall, with large dreamy eyes that held shining sparks when she laughed, and brown hair with a curl in it, and teeth that seemed more like a first set than a second, they were so small and even. The outside of her might have belonged indifferently to north, south, east or west, but the inside of her was Celtic to the core. Both Irish and Highland blood ran in her veins, and unknown ancestors had handed down their heritage of laughter and tears, that joyous zest for life and keen intensity of feeling, that fairy glamour which may transfigure the commonest things, or beguile the heart to waste its devotion upon trifles, which is the birthright of those whose forbears, in the dim forgotten twilight of our island's history, kept their courts at Tara and Camelot and left their wealth of legend behind them.

Sometime in this period Angela must have come across the story of Hy Brazil, the 'fairy island' which she liked to think was the source of her name, and which prompted her to alter the pronunciation. (She told the story as 'The Storm Sprite' in 1903 in *Our School Magazine.*) Edward MacLysaght, the authority on Irish names, does not concur. In his definitive work, *The Surnames of Ireland*, published by the Irish University Press, he gives a possible derivation from *bres*, meaning strife, not only for Brazil but for Brassil and O'Breasail.

Angela preferred to believe that the Blessed Isle, off the coast of Donegal, 'deep in the roots of Celtic mythology', was the origin, an Atlantic Shangri-La which generally

vanished when you steered for it, but occasionally some favoured mortal would manage to land on its golden shore, and there he found an idyllic country, where there was neither death nor pain nor sin, naught save immortal and unfading youth and endless joy. Its people, beautiful as the gods, were of a higher race, and greatly skilled in medicine, and so much would they impart of their lore that the few travellers who returned to Ireland could exercise wonderful powers of healing, and were called 'Brazil' or 'blessed' ever afterwards.

By the time Angela and Walter took up residence in Coventry in 1911 they had made the phonetic switch.

[7]
PATRIOTIC
SCHOOLGIRLS

Clarence Brazil died on the twenty-first of September, 1899, which was the year that Angela achieved her first publication, *The Mischievous Brownie*, four children's plays under the imprint of T. W. Paterson of Edinburgh. The slight volume cost threepence, and the content was a mixture of archness, sophistication and *grand guignol*. The ogre's gruesome menu in *The Enchanted Fiddle* consisted of Ploughboy Soup, Filleted Sailors' Soles, Fried Fingers on Toast, Roast Shopkeeper, Bishop's Brain with Potatoes, Schoolboy's Cheek with Sauce and Maiden's Lips with Sugar and Cream. In *The Wishing Princess* – she had been given the gift of unalterable wishes by her fairy godmother – the King introduced the awful Tormentilla to her new teachers.

'This is Professor Torkenuff, D.D., who will instruct you in the dead languages, moral philosophy, theology, biology, phrenology, entomology, conchology, physiology and zoology.'

Tormentilla responded by wishing them handless, headless, deaf, blind, dumb and immovable with babies' brains and the ability to say only 'goo-goo' and 'baba goes by-byes'. She had, however, a final redeeming wish that her godmother recall the gift. It was an odd collection but then Angela had not yet found her *métier*.

She wrote the plays in Wales, where she had made friends with

every school-girl I met, and we always found much to talk about. Children were the dearest of companions: I had many small chums at Llanbedr, and we did all kinds of delightful things together. We had picnics on the hills, and once we had a supper-party in the woods beside the stream, with a bonfire, and

Chinese lanterns hanging among the trees. On wet days they would run to our house in mackintoshes, and I would tell them stories in the barn, sitting upon the hay.

Family and friends suggested that Angela should write a novel, but her oral story-telling convinced her that she had found her audience, and when on Clarence's death Angelica sold the cottage and bought a converted farmhouse in the same village, Angela claimed the garden studio for her study. She worked mainly in the evenings, using a notebook and pencil, consigning much paper to the log fire, and in the day she wrote, when the weather was fine, in the open air, beside the stream. She would complete two or three chapters in draft form and then read them aloud to Amy and Angelica who pounced on the split infinitives. She wrote *The Fortunes of Philippa* three times before she submitted it.

There were residential changes, too, during Mr Brazil's lifetime. Son Clarence had moved away from home and was practising as a solicitor in Dalton-in-Furness in Lancaster by the time Walter qualified and was ready to set up in practice. (He obtained his B.Sc. in Manchester, his London M.B. at Barts in 1889 – the year he published his first paper in the British Medical Journal* – and his M.D. in 1891. He also acquired a Cambridge D.P.H. in 1892.) In 1893 or 1894 the Brazils sold the family house, Walter either bought or rented 365 Burnside, Blackburn Road, in Bolton Le Moors, and Angela returned from London to housekeep for him. It is probable that Angelica, Clarence senior and Amy moved to 14 Bangor Street, since the 1898 Directory for Bolton records a Mrs Brazil living at the address.

Angelica was Clarence's only beneficiary. His estate was valued at £3,092 6s. 8d., which was equivalent to £37,000 in 1975. The new cottage, Ffynnonbedr (it meant Peter's Well; Llanbedr is St Peter's Church) now served as a return-base between the travels upon which the three Brazil women embarked and which are dated not by the journals they must surely have kept but by Amy's china. From the paintings she made on her foreign excursions she would, on her homecoming, reduce one to miniature on the centre of a plate, saucer or cup, and over the years built up an entire service which she displayed on the velvet-padded shelves of the cottage dresser. From it we know that they were in Rome, Venice and Pompeii in 1903; in Egypt and Nazareth – possibly with Walter who at some time made the pilgrimage – in 1904 (Angela's

* 'The Normal Thoracle Resonances in Left-handed Persons.'

account of 'A Winter in Palestine' was published in *Burgon's Magazine* in 1905); in Sicily and Ireland in 1907 (she used the Irish background in 1910 when she was writing *The New Girl at St Chad's*); the Tyrol in 1908, and in Bordighera, Perinaldo and Arles in 1909. Walter gave up his practice in 1908, and in 1911 *Nisbet's Medical Dictionary* gave his address as Ffynnonbedr, North Wales, and referred to his late appointment as house surgeon at the Manchester Royal Infirmary, accounting for the two intervening years.

For some time Amy was the district nurse at Llanbedr, and Carol Walters (Leila's daughter) remembers the story of a dark winter night when Amy was called out to attend a birth at a remote mountain cottage, where, much to her distress, the baby was born blind. In 1911, Walter bought the successful practice of Dr Milner-Moore of Coventry, and with Angela again to keep house he moved to 1 The Quadrant, the end house of an early Victorian crescent in the city's most exclusive residential area. Amy took a nursing post at the Stratford-upon-Avon hospital (in due course Walter was appointed Opthalmic Surgeon there) and lived at Stratford with Angelica, near to both family and work. When Angelica died in 1915 she left Ffynnonbedr to Amy, who then joined her brother and sister at The Quadrant, completing the 'holy trinity' which was to influence the local artistic and social life for years to come.

Angelica's death in 1915 shattered them all. She was eighty but had remained active and extraordinarily youthful and energetic until the previous summer. 'With the hot July weather,' wrote Angela in *The Luckiest Girl in the School*,

> Aunt Harriet's health flagged. The erect figure stooped a little, her high colour had faded and her voice lost some of its energy and determination . . . she fretted greatly at the enforced inaction. She was one of those characters who would rather wear out than rust out, and it required the utmost firmness on the part of her doctor to persuade her from over-exerting herself.

Gilbert Morris (who as professional child pianist was known as M. A. Gilbert and later, as pianist and composer took the name of A. Morris-Gilbert) was a schoolboy of twelve when he came into the lives of the Brazils two years earlier and, although he had not known her well, he cried when he heard of Angelica's death. He had spent a holiday with her and Amy at Weston-super-Mare and said: 'She was wonderful with young people, having remained young so long herself.' Knowing Angela's tendency to take immediate experiences and her reactions to them and to adapt her plots around them, it is likely that Angelica not only generated Aunt Harriet, but marked (as Aunt Harriet did) a small volume of extracts with a pencilled cross at the lines 'For I'm old, alone and tired,/And my long life's work is done'.

'How horribly we live right inside ourselves!' thought Winona. 'How few people know just what we're feeling and thinking, and how hard it is to let them know! The "I" at the back of me is so different from the outside of me . . . we all live in our own little world and only touch one another now and then.'

The family was reduced in size both by Angelica's death and by Clarence's marriage. Amy and Angelica had never wavered in their affection, but Clarence damned himself utterly in Angela's eyes when he married a woman twenty years his junior and socially beneath him. She probably condemned him for marrying at all.

Florence Snozwell was the sister of a piano manufacturer and both Angela and Walter denied any knowledge of the firm, even when confronted with the evidence that they knew it very well indeed. They felt that their infant nephew, John Walter, was tainted by his mother's birth, and Angela worked out her feelings by denigrating Florence and all but canonizing Jackie in *A Patriotic Schoolgirl*. She turned Florence into a barmaid (the lowest and most vulgar situation she could think of),* and Jackie, who was an invalid, into an angelic child in a spinal carriage who loved only his aunt. Thinly disguised as Eric, he met Marjorie, Dona and Elaine one afternoon on a cliff walk. (The italics are all mine!)

On the road above stood an invalid carriage, piled up with innumerable parcels, and containing also a small boy. He was a charmingly pretty little fellow, with a very pale, delicately oval face, beautiful pathetic brown eyes, and rich golden hair that fell in curls over his shoulders like a girl's.

As soon as the attendant, who 'wasn't tidy enough for a nurse', wheeled the child away, the girls began to speculate.

* A particularly vicious barb since Florence was gentle, quiet and refined to the point of wearing a hat and gloves even when going out to post a letter. Like Clarence she had no time for the family affectations and continued to call herself Braz*il*.

86

'Poor wee chap! I wonder what's the matter with him?' said Elaine when the long perambulator had turned the corner. 'And I wonder where he can possibly be going? There are no houses that way – only a wretched little village with a few cottages.'

'I can't place him at all,' replied Marjorie. *'He's not a poor person's child, and he's not exactly a gentleman's.'*

On a second, deliberate meeting, when the girls had given him a book, he offered friendship.

'I've got names for you all,' he said shyly. 'I made them up while I was in bed. You,' pointing to Elaine, 'are Princess Goldilocks; and you,' with a finger at Marjorie and Dona, 'are two fairies, Bluebell and Silverstar. No, I don't want to know your real names; I like make-up ones better. We always play fairies when Titania comes to see me.'

'Who's Titania?'

'She's my Auntie. She's the very loveliest person in all the world.'

Titania turned out eventually to be none other than strict but likeable Miss Norton of Brackenfield College, misjudged by her pupils, who had not known the burden of love she carried.

'I didn't know it was you two who have been so kind to Eric. I should like to explain about him, and then you'll understand. *My eldest brother married very much beneath him . . .* I can't bear to think of Eric being brought up in such surroundings . . . I had planned that when he is a little older I would try to persuade them to let me send him to a good preparatory school, but now' – her voice broke – 'it is not a question of education, but whether he will grow up at all.'

Jack Brazil grew for another eight years after *A Patriotic Schoolgirl* and reached the age of sixteen. He had, his mother said, 'all the Brazil brains rolled into one'. In the family tradition he was an ardent Egyptologist, and when Angela or Walter arranged for a professor to talk to him, they disputed, and it was Jack who was proved to be right. He faced his death with equanimity. During his last meeting with Gilbert Morris in Polperro he said: 'You know I'm going to die? I'm not afraid. It will be wonderful. I doubt if we shall meet again.' He was the last of the legitimate line, and if there was any other issue, Angela never publicly acknowledged it, making sure there was no evidence to support the claim but induction and instinct, all of which I shall come to in its chronological place.

A Patriotic Schoolgirl was not published until 1917, but by the time Angela moved to The Quadrant she had (at the age of forty-two) already established her reputation.

In 1904 *A Terrible Tomboy* had received favourable notices. The *Scotsman* described it as 'a delightful book for young people ... very amusing and enjoyable'; the *Yorkshire Observer* said it was 'a charming story' which would 'give delight to hundreds of young girls', and the *Manchester Guardian* pronounced that 'there is more humour and less sentiment in this clever book than we have found in most new stories of the kind'. In 1906 *The Fortunes of Philippa* launched her as a writer of school stories, and Blackie's commissioned *The Third Class at Miss Kay's* in 1908, *The Nicest Girl in the School* in 1909 (the same year that Nelson's published *Bosom Friends*), *The Manor House School* in 1910, and two books, *The New Girl at St Chad's* and *A Fourth Form Friendship* in 1911. She had also been contributing regularly to *Little Folks, The Girls' Realm* and *The British Girls' Annual.* (Walter's literary contribution had been two further papers, 'Case of Small White Kidney' and 'A Graphic Method of Recording Heart Cases', both in the *Medical Chronicle* in 1901.)

Shortly after the move, the Brazils arranged for a family pew at St Michael's Church, which was later to become Coventry Cathedral, and all three joined the Natural History and Scientific Society which had been inaugurated only two years before. In 1914 Walter was elected as one of the Vice-Presidents and Angela onto the committee, and they remained active members until the Second World War, with Walter becoming President and Angela the first woman Vice-President.

It is remarkable that Angela's prolific output of books and articles, together with her extensive travels, should have allowed her time for abundant committee work and society activities. Her participation was wholehearted, as the minutes reveal; she attended soirées and lectures ('The lecturer illustrated his lecture with a series of coloured slides, the beauty of which, and of a nightingale's song played on a gramophone, were highly appreciated by the audience'); she contributed sketches and entered competitions which she frequently won. She came first in the Identification of Inaccurate Pictures, first in the Identification of Natural Objects, and organized other competitions for schoolchildren, many of whom are adult members of the society today. She tramped forth on rambles (tea at the Royal Oak Rooms afterwards followed by a musical evening) and read papers. On 12 January 1914 she entertained members with 'Poet's Corner in Lakeland', and 'the paper was much enhanced by a series of water-colour sketches of the district from the brush of Miss (Amy) Brazil'. On 15 December 1915 she delivered 'Flowers and Folk-lore' (Walter was in the chair), which linked the close relationship of flowers to religious worship and sacred festivals and credited others with assorted virtues. The piece was published years afterwards in Blackie's *Girls' Annual*. Among a variety of visiting speakers, Walter talked on 'Prehistoric Dwellings', giving, so the proceedings record, 'a short (!) account of the earth's cosmogony, showing how various species of plants and animals were charac-teristic of certain epochs, and laying special emphasis on the development and gradual recession of the great continental glaciers as determining the different types of shelter to which man had resorted'. Evenings ended often at the Geisha Café in Hert-ford Street, which was the rendezvous that Egbert Saxon chose to take his sister Ingred to tea in *A Popular Schoolgirl*, where it became the Alhambra.

When you have tea every day at a long table full of girls, the meal is apt to grow monotonous, and it was a welcome change to take it instead in a gay Oriental room with Moorish decora-tions . . . Ingred leaned back on an embroidered cushion and ate cakes covered with pink sugar, and listened to a violin solo.

The society's winter programmes included the fortnightly lectures and an occasional ramble, but the summer was the time for the members to set out on regular walks. There were two which were especially memorable, one to the woodlands of Brownshill Green (when Walter 'called attention to the burring cry of the nightjar or goatsucker which could be heard in the woodlands, and where, in the heart of the wood, the party met the Reverend Archdeacon Bree, of Allesley, with whom the entomologists had a most interesting conversation'), and another later in the same season when members took the train to Kenilworth. En route 'Dr Brazil pointed out some fine specimens of the Twayblade on the railway bank'. There was a thunderstorm at Aschow and tea in 'an old timbered cottage'.

In October that year, 1916, the highest accolade was bestowed by the society on the Brazils, or perhaps the accolade was bestowed by the Brazils upon the society. Only four years after their arrival in the city the annual *conversazione* was held at The Quadrant.

There were sixty guests, including the mayor, and in his address Walter said that the society brought various classes of people together, and united them in a common purpose, by a process of levelling up, not down; 'for nature seems to raise all who come into contact with her'. It was a sentiment with which Angela agreed, providing that it did not extend beyond the agreed boundaries, and certainly not into the bosom of one's own family!

The entertainments that evening comprised a lantern lecture on 'The Solitary Mud Wasp', two 'novel nature competitions' devised by Angela, a show of exhibits (they included some of Angela's drawings of flowering plants and a Killerny Fern found by Walter) and a musical interlude which, I have reason to believe, was performed by young Gilbert Morris, who was pressed into service at many of the Brazil's social gatherings.

There is no book of Angela's in which 'nature' does not have an integrated part. The long walking tour in *A Popular Schoolgirl* had its origin in the exploits of the Coventry Natural History and Scientific Society. Like the Kenilworth ramble, the participants set off by train, and then under the leadership of Miss Strong, 'who had some experience of mountaineering in Switzerland', the girls of Grovebury thrilled to the spring air,

> that resurrection of Nature when the thralldom of winter is over, and beauty comes back to the grey dim world. The old Greeks felt it thousands of years ago, and fabled it in their myth of Persephone and her return from Hades. The Druids knew it in Ancient Britain, and fixed their religious ceremonies for May Day. The birds were carolling it still in the hedgerows, and the girls caught the joyous infection and danced along in defiance of Miss Strong's jog-trot guide walk. Even the mistress herself, so wise at the outset, finally flung prudence to the winds, and skirmished through the coppices with enthusiasm equal to that of her pupils, lured from the pathway by glimpses of kingcups, or the pursuit of a Peacock butterfly.

The ramble had its tense moments. Bess and Ingred had an argument over a blue flower 'plainly of the labiate species', when Bess insisted that it was a bugle and Ingred replied scornfully that it was self-heal. Miss Strong put the matter crushingly right.

'Bugle, certainly,' she declared emphatically. 'The first bit we've found this year. It's out early. Self-heal? Oh dear no! The two are rather alike and are sometimes mistaken one for another, but no botanist would dream of confusing them. Bugle is a spring and early summer flower, and self-heal blooms much later. Make a note in your nature diaries that you found bugle on 15th April.'

Angela herself was given a handsome nature diary by one of her schoolgirl friends that year, and she kept it for the rest of her life so that entries for five or six different and non-consecutive years often occurred on one page. She recorded not only her own finds, but Walter's too. Friends contributed. Leila, writing to her in 1930, included a specimen of Andromeda. 'I dare say you have already seen it but we found it on a peat bog near here and I was *very* delighted, it is new to me. I even dared a big bull to go – at least he suddenly stepped out of a hollow behind us and cut off our retreat so I had to go on!'

As Angela and Walter grew older he did not always go on the rambles, but would collect Angela in his car so that she did not have to walk home. If there were children taking part they were offered lifts back to Coventry, and Walter's driving has been conversely described both as very sedate and wildly dangerous. He was among the avant-garde of local doctors in owning a car, although his bicycle still stood in the hall of The Quadrant in 1916. An early blurred photograph shows him sitting in his first car, a black Ford tourer. The 'little yellow Deemster' driven by Dr Tremayne in *A Fortunate Term* took the Brazils to Cornwall in 1921. Later he drove a small, black, Morris Cowley saloon.

An important offshoot of the Coventry Natural History and Scientific Society was the inception of the City Guild, in which Angela was involved. Her passion for botany was equalled only by her romantic fascination with antiquity, and on 26 May 1914, a meeting was held at three o'clock in the mayoress's parlour.

'It has been thought desirable', said the leaflet announcing the occasion, 'to form a Society on the lines of the S.O.A. Guild to preserve those antiquities of Coventry which are not under the care of the Corporation and to influence, where possible, the artistic development of the City.' In June Angela was elected as Honorable Secretary, and the aims and objects were properly defined and set down in print. Among them were the scheduling and preservation of buildings, the organization of lectures and exhibitions, and, 'bearing in mind the delicate relationship of the rights of the individual to the common weal – and that "an Englishman's house is his castle", the Society will rely chiefly on the moral suasion and a friendly indication of what seems to them "A Better Way"' – a style of phrasing that indicates it was Angela's composition.

The Guild did not waste time. By the beginning of July the executive council had lodged a protest with the city council concerning the neglect of historic Butcher Row and Little Palace Yard. Hints of rivalry between Angela and fellow-member Miss Dormer Harris have filtered down the decades. Certainly Miss Dormer Harris contributed an article to *Country Life* in March 1915, relating the activities of the Guild, but in April the subcommittee met at The Quadrant, with Angela as hostess, to discuss the site of the proposed museum, a cherished aim.

The Brazil home was not unlike a museum itself. Walter was the serious collector, with an inordinate number of antique clocks which struck and chimed all over the house, punctuating every gathering noisily and variously at each quarter hour. He was an authority and published a small pamphlet for the museum which the Guild was to instigate in due course. He also bought guns, swords and musical instruments. He was particularly proud of a spinet reputed to have belonged to Pepys (somewhere in the diary he mentioned how he had paid £25 for one) and an old vielle or hurdy-gurdy, shaped like a mandolin, with a small wheel at one end for the right hand and a few keys on the body for the left. This instrument, or one exactly like it, was the subject of Schubert's 'Hurdy-Gurdy Song', which the doctor would render to his guests in (as the years passed) an increasingly quavering voice. There was scarcely an empty surface. Besides the clocks there were prized botanical specimens, including stuffed animals and cases of butterflies, on display. Amy and Angela, magpies rather than connoisseurs, brought home tourist junk from their travels and stood it on every available table, shelf and ledge. The walls were covered with paintings and sketches by all three Brazils, although mainly Amy's, and with paintings by friends. Amy was a member of the Coventry and Warwickshire Society of Artists and her paintings were exhibited not only on the home walls but at local exhibitions. Angela, who fought Walter for the right to privacy with a 'boudoir', had her own private collections of early children's books (now in the City Library's Local Studies department) and tear-bottles. The furniture was varied in its period, and mainly dark, ranging from the high-backed, hard-seated oak seventeenth-century chairs in the doctor's surgery on the ground floor to the Victoriana elsewhere. Abe Jephcott's poem of worship (Appendix B) reveals his own state of ecstasy rather than the actuality of the furnishings: the 'inlay of pearl, the porcelain, the jade,/Riches in pictures and caskets antique' was less accurate than 'Old dressers in oak and craftwork in teak'.

It is not surprising to learn that the first gifts to the Guild Museum included several items from the Brazils. The initial batch, which preceded the premises, comprised a pair of gloves worn by George Eliot, mouldings and carvings and some dolls circa 1839.

Angela, of course, was on the museum committee, and in 1916 an unsigned article in the local paper pressed the suitability of the crypt of Coventry's medieval Guildhall of St Mary's as the best available site.

The war slowed the progress of such peaceable activities, but the Guild continued to function, and took over the tenancy of Little Palace Yard, letting it out as allotments, an event which was transmuted into the 'Back to the Land Girls' from Brackenfield in *A Patriotic Schoolgirl*: 'They rolled and marked the tennis courts, earthed up potatoes, put sticks for the peas, planted out cabbages, and weeded the drive.'

Of the gardening at Palace Yard, Angela wrote in the minutes: 'It has now been dug up and planted with vegetables, and presents a very creditable appearance as a war garden, in striking contrast to its former deplorable conditions of neglect.' To a schoolgirl correspondent she replied: 'It is useful for you to be fond of gardening in the present time, isn't it?'

Angela herself did not Dig for Victory, but she worked in the local crèche, sharing the experience with Avelyn soon afterwards in *For the School Colours*.

Out at the front our boys were fighting for Britain's honour, but their heroism would be of no avail if the hands slacked that forged the weapons at home. The workers who made the munitions, and those who toiled to feed the workers and keep them fit, were taking their share of the burden, and, in however small and obscure a way, were pushing the world on towards the victory of Right over Might . . .

This day nursery had been opened in order that women who

wished to help at munitions might leave their babies to be taken care of while they were at work.

There were limits to the effects of war which Angela could portray for her readers; she was after all writing for girls between twelve and sixteen, but she imparted the contemporary jingoism with style.

They sewed national costumes for the Serbians, rolled bandages at the War Supply Depot, distributed dinners at the municipal kitchens, taught gymnastic classes at the girls' clubs, visited crippled children, got up concerts for wounded soldiers, and organised Christmas parties for slum babies.

These were the war activities which no doubt directly involved Angela in Coventry; apart from her other altruistic interests, she was elected on to the Y.W.C.A. Committee in 1914. Wounded soldiers, like Winona's brother Percy Woodward, were drawn from the young men nursed by Amy and treated by Walter.

'I first met them when I returned as a badly wounded officer from Gallipoli and hospitals in 1916,' Major George Moore wrote to me of the Brazils. He was a patient of Walter's and remembered him as 'a courtly gentleman' who was 'always dressed in dark formal clothes and had a charming manner ... the doctor was highly respected, and was very kind when he attended my mother in her last illness'. A. Morris-Gilbert, who knew him well, said: 'He was a most devoted medico, and I can never remember him hesitating for a moment when a call came, even in the midst of dinner, party or whatever. I can remember when he sat two days and two nights with one patient and was rewarded. The patient lived to a ripe old age.' The doctors in Angela's books are all equally dedicated.

Angela must have met many girls at the Y.W.C.A. whose sweethearts and brothers were killed or wounded. Her readers told her of their personal tragedies and triumphs. 'My father is a soldier in the Royal Engineers and expects to sail for German East Africa any day now,' said one proudly. 'One of my brother's friends was killed ... Major Godden ... he was the first Englishman to loop the loop in the dark,' wrote another. Molly Alford of Camberley, Surrey, told Angela that she was looking forward to Christmas

because my Auntie from Windermere is going to spend it with us. But it will be a very sad one because we have lost such a lot of friends. A great friend of ours was reported missing, believed killed, now reported killed but we are still hoping he *may* be a prisoner. He was only 20 and such a nice looking boy with a mop of curls which he 'plastered' down. Ken's real friend was killed in June poor fellow and another poor boy soon after. It *is* awful. Oh! how I wish it were over.

More optimistic and extrovert, Dorothy Abbot from Finchley wrote to her favourite author:

> Is it cheeky of me to write? I felt I had to. Do you know the feeling? I expect you think I am a swanky customer – otherwise an Indian girl. But I am not. I am Scotch-Irish.
> P.S. I have discovered I want to tell you heaps more. (I have just noticed that I've used 46 I's, isn't that dreadful!!) It was about my lonely soldier, everyone knows about him, he's my special War Charge. I write to him and send him parcels. It's so nice to think I've got something to do in the war.

The girls wrote of their fathers and brothers in hospital and at the front. Whether any of them joined Winona in her enthusiasm for a return to the trenches is an open question.

> Dearly as she had always loved the old Percy, she felt the new one she had met today had the makings of a stronger and finer character than she had ever dared to hope.
> 'The Commandant gives an excellent report of him,' said Miss Beach. 'I asked her particularly if there were any likelihood of his remaining lame, but she says not. The surgeon declares he'll have him back in the trenches in the autumn.'
> 'How glorious! Percy's just wild to go back. I believe he'll do something splendid, and get a commission, or perhaps win the Victoria Cross!'

The armistice was signed, but Angela's girls were reluctant to give up the patriotic activities they had enjoyed so much. In *A Popular Schoolgirl* Lispeth Scott made a speech which managed to gather several of Angela's hobby-horses into a single stable.

> 'You're all in new forms, and I'm the new Head Prefect. It's not only in school that everything's different, but in the world

95

outside as well. This is our first term since peace was signed. I can remember our first term after war was declared. I was only in IIIa then – quite a youngster! Hetty Hughes, who was head girl, made a speech, and told us what we ought to do to try to help our country. I think some of us who were here have never forgotten that. We nearly hurrahed the roof off, and we formed a Knitting Club and a Soldier's Parcel Society on the spot. Well, today the Empire is at peace, but our country needs our help as much as ever, or even more. It's making a fresh start, and we want the new world to be a better place than the old. Hundreds of thousands of gallant young lives have been gladly given to establish this new world – in this school alone we know to our cost – and we owe it to our heroic dead not to let their sacrifice be in vain. We want a better and purer England to rise up and make a clean sweep of the bad things that disgraced her before. I expect you'll say: "Oh, that's for politicians and not for us schoolgirls!" but it isn't. Popular opinion is a mighty thing. The schoolgirls of today are the women of tomorrow and the women of a country have an enormous amount to do with the formation of public opinion – more nowadays than ever before – and their influence will go on increasing with every year that passes. If each of us tried to help the world instead of hindering it, think what an asset each one may be to the country! It's really a tremendous honour to know that we can all take part in the reconstruction of England. It's like being allowed to lay a brick in the foundation of a new building. Of course you'll ask me: "Well, and how are we going to help?" That's just what I want to talk about. We pride ourselves on being practical at the College. Some of us thought we might start a new society, to be called "The Rainbow League". It's a sort of "Guild of Helpers", and we want to do all kinds of jolly things to help in the town, something like our old "Knitting Club" and "Soldier's Parcel Society", only of course different. We could give concerts, and make clothes for war orphans, and toys for the hospitals, and scrapbooks for crippled children. There are heaps of nice things that you'll just love doing. It's called "The Rainbow League", because a rainbow was set in the sky after the Flood, to help people to remember, and we want, in our small way, not to let the Great War be forgotten, but to do our bit to help the future of the race.'

Together with the other prefects, Lispeth handed out typewritten sheets of paper which set out the aims of the league, rather as the progenitors of the City Guild had compiled their list in 1914. These were less practical, however, and had a lofty moral tone.

That every girl must do her best to help all other girls, and to advance the Sisterhood of women.

That woman's greatest and strongest weapons are love and sweetness.

That by conscious radiation of unselfish love to her fellow beings, a girl may undoubtedly raise the moral atmosphere of the world around her.

That every girl, however young, can help this glorious old country, and that, joined together for good, the schoolgirls of a nation can influence the well-being of a race.

That good can always triumph over evil, and that love and unselfishness will wipe out many social blots, and put beauty in their place.

In spite of new movements in every branch of the arts which permeated even drawing-room decor, Angela appeared to remain unaware of such developments. Just as she had ignored the pacifist movement or the intellectual arguments for it, so she made no mention of Picasso, Stravinsky or Joyce (while constantly citing earlier artists) or even the Bloomsbury Group which was centred around her London base, the Kenilworth Hotel.

Meanwhile, back in Coventry, the members of the City Guild at last acquired the crypt of St Mary's Hall for their museum!

[8]
ANGELA
ENTERTAINS

From its beginnings in the crypt, the museum moved upstairs where it could be opened to the public. By a strategically contrived misunderstanding the exhibits were put into two rooms directly below those actually given by the city council, which had difficult access only by a small spiral staircase. Nothing was said by the authorities, and in due course, following a meeting at The Quadrant, admission prices were fixed and the doors were unlocked to reveal the treasures collected during the war years and until now unseen in the crypt. Parties of not less than twelve schoolchildren were allowed in at 1d. each.

It was on one of these wet Fridays that Miss Chatham suggested taking the Sixth Form to see the City Museum. This was a new development in Kingfield and had lately been opened. It occupied a large room in the old Guild Hall, and was only about five minutes from the school. The Sixth joyfully snatched the opportunity offered to them, put away books, tools, and other impediments, and went to the cloakroom to change their shoes. Then minutes later a jolly-looking party, with mackintoshes and umbrellas, followed Miss Chatham down the High Street to the Guild Hall. They went under the ancient archway, and across the courtyard, and through the old doorway, and up the oak stairs, and along the tapestried corridor into the great central hall, hung with armour and weapons of bygone Kingfield citizens. From this hall led many thick oak doors, and one, under the minstrels' gallery, gave access to the new museum. It was a fairly large room, built like the rest of the Guild Hall in a medieval fashion, with sandstone walls, a carved roof, and latticed windows. It held a number of show-cases containing various exhibits.

Was the friendly 'lady curator', who encouraged Lesbia and Marion to stay after the rest of the class, a version of Angela herself? Did she create the 'adventure' from some real incident when two enthusiastic schoolgirls stayed behind for a private view of the exhibits? Lesbia and Marion (in *Loyal to the School*) were anxious to see the illuminated manuscripts in the stockroom. It had not occurred to Miss Renton, the curator, that the caretaker would lock them in.

Marion was dabbing her eyes openly. She made no pretence at heroism. Adventures might be romantic enough in the Middle Ages, but they were decidedly unpleasant in the twentieth century. She would rather read about them than experience them.

Leaving her chum to be consoled by Miss Renton, Lesbia mounted the chair and looked through the window. About three feet below her there was a fairly broad ledge, which adjoined a roof to the right. After all, the opening was not so very small.

'I believe I could squeeze through here,' she volunteered.

In 1922 the museum moved to better premises at the Old Bablake School; in 1923 Angela presented a new showcase; on 26 May 1924 she read a report on the occasion of the tenth birthday of the Guild.

'In conclusion,' she said, 'may I urge the claims of the museum as a factor in the education of the young? Only last week I took a party of twenty-six schoolgirls round the showcases and was greatly pleased by the intelligent interest they displayed. They were much attracted by the specimens of ancient pottery and glass excavated in Coventry, and also by the prehistoric weapons, which illustrated their school history lessons. They eagerly examined the pictures of vanished Coventry and compared them with present-day streets, and would no doubt take home many new ideas in connection with the story of their native place.'

As a result, an Education Week was planned, when the museum would be free, and at the back of the Minutes Book is an entry in Angela's handwriting which reads very like the lists she made for the fictional dormitory feasts: 'At annual meeting used $\frac{3}{4}$ lb. coffee, 1 lb. lump sugar, about 1 lb. fancy biscuits. China hired from co-operative bakery, Cox Street.'

In 1930 the corporation took over the responsibility of the museum from the City Guild and in this way it became the direct ancestor of the present Civic Herbert Museum in Bayley Lane.

From the beginning of the century Angela and Amy had given children's parties and both contrived and entered into any event which involved the young. Carol Walters (then Carol Samuels) and Mary Hunter were both children in Llanbedr when 'The Pageant' took place in 1906 in the grounds of Caerhun Hall. The actual rehearsing of the dances (there was a group of fairies and a group of butterflies) took place on the Brazil's lawn at Ffynnonbedr, and Amy and Angela painted the butterfly wings for the costumes. 'They were very beautiful,' said Mary Hunter. Angela also made a Beast's head, with terrifying open jaws and phosphorescent eyes, and there is a local story that she put it on and hid in the back of the cattle barn in order to frighten the farmer, Mr Hughes.

The centrepiece of the pageant was the crowning of the Rose Queen, who was the daughter of the Hall. Carol was Britannia, and the Boy Scouts followed behind her in the procession. The Brazil sisters enjoyed it as much as the children.

As soon as she was settled in Coventry, Angela made herself known at the local girls' schools. She was well placed at The Quadrant. At the other end of the short terrace, in the penultimate house, Miss Hales (a fellow member of the City Guild committee) ran The Quadrant High School. She was a non-militant suffragette (although the school was essentially for 'young ladies') and Angela shared many of her views. She seemed to have been granted the freedom of the school by Miss Hales, for she dropped in from time to time, listened to lessons, chatted to the girls at playtime and occasionally would go up to the Coventry and North Warwick sports ground to watch the hockey. In 1918 she offered a prize for a letter written by one schoolgirl to another describing the hockey match played between The Quadrant and Leamington High School. She incorporated the letter in *A Popular Schoolgirl*, prefaced by italics: *This letter is an account of a real match, written by a real schoolgirl.* The real captain, Margaret Webster, became Blossom Webster, for names were the only alterations Angela made.

Blossom and Veronica were once more bullying off. This time the latter was the quicker of the two, for, with a clever hit, she succeeded in sending the ball away to her Left Wing . . . Of course Ingred was the heroine of the hour. As she was being escorted to the pavilion, flushed but triumphant, Miss Giles said to her: 'Well played! I am proud of you!'

It might have been written by Angela herself. The book was bound in pale grey with a blue and yellow edging – the colours of The Quadrant High School.

There were two other small schools close at hand. The Misses Bottomley (Ethel and Evelyn), themselves daughters of a Methodist minister, were the joint principals of Cheshunt School, and at the age of ten most of their pupils, due to the excellent grounding, went on to Leamington High School, passing the entrance examination with ease. The rival establishment was Queen's Road School, under the direction of Miss Flinn, who had once been a very good violinist. Both catered for the rising professional class, and bankers, doctors and ministers sent their daughters to one or the other establishment when they were five or six years old. There were uniform gymslips, navy knickers and summer dresses. From the age of ten, black stockings were compulsory.

Doreen Corbett, a Cheshunt girl, remembers Angela at summer Open Afternoons, touring the schoolrooms, looking at the scrapbooks and the modelling exhibits, taking tea, with strawberries and cream and fancy cakes, in the garden. She wore skirts that were long for the fashion of the time (they were currently ascending) and her dresses were soft and loose, mauve and pinky-mauve, made of chiffon or voile. She always had bows on her shoes and straw hats adorned by flowers. To the children she seemed old and venerable, although she was only in her late forties, and Doreen thought she had a curious sallow skin, and was reminded of a water spaniel. She recalls that Angela had dark hair turning to grey, a slightly bulbous nose, and spoke in a soft contralto, never raising her voice. She appeared to be vague, but in fact she observed with sharp eyes and open ears, just as she did on those mornings when she caught the school train to Leamington, solely to watch and listen to the commuting girls.

Doreen also attended Angela's winter parties – or at least, some of Angela's winter parties, because there were many, and they were divided by class and situation with characteristic rigidity. All of them, however, were equally enjoyable.

Doreen and her younger sister, Diana, received their yearly

invitations by way of parental approach, and there was always a to-do about the party dresses. Girls (it was *de rigueur*) wore white with coloured sashes. The dresses were trimmed with stiff *broderie anglaise*, which meant enduring the discomfort of the starched hems rubbing against bare knees. There were white socks, of course, and pumps, and before the departure to The Quadrant there were maternal lectures on the correct behaviour at the tea-table. It absolutely would not do to make a *faux pas* at The Quadrant.

At that time there were certainly two and possibly three maids at the house. Under supervision of the parlour-maid, the little girls changed from their outdoor shoes into their party pumps, and as soon as the last guests had arrived they went into the dark dining-room for tea.

Buns, chocolate biscuits, table-creams, jellies, and a decorated Christmas cake (recollects Doreen Corbett) with weak, possibly China tea, served for those who were sufficiently sophisticated, in fragile cups. There was milk and lemonade for those who still had nursery palates. The maids, Amy and Angela all attended at the table. As the meal drew to a close, Dr Brazil might make a brief appearance.

After tea the party moved upstairs. Primed in advance, the children had prepared recitations or songs or music, for performance was implicit in the invitation and occasioned sinking hearts in the bosoms of the less extrovert guests. They sat in a circle, cross-legged, skirts carefully arranged, and lots were drawn. Doreen won the prize on one occasion, when she recited a poem called 'Draughts and Dominoes', which she had found in an annual.

Little Tommy Timbertoes among his other feats
Once ate a bag of dominoes – he thought that they were sweets.
They gave him such a dreadful pain, the worst he'd ever felt,
And where he felt the pain the most was where he wore his belt.

Tommy died in the end, because the draughts of castor oil and squills combined disastrously with the dominoes, but Angela was very amused. Another year the prize was won by a girl who daringly sang 'Tiptoe through the Tulips'. When the performances were over Angela dextrously rolled cottonwool snowballs, embellished with bells or holly, across the floor for the guests to intercept and catch. Each snowball contained a present, a hat and a motto. Once the winning performer was rolled an *orange* snowball. Inside was a little glass book, the size of a fingernail, attached to a ring so that it could be worn on a chain or a ribbon.

'In my next book look for your own name,' said Angela to Doreen at one Christmas party (which she did. It was *Joan's Best Chum*). The Mavis and Merle books were Doreen's favourites and Angela inscribed one, 'From your friend, Angela Brazil'. She was always writing down names in her little red book. Noelle Osmond, who published her own short memoir of Angela in 1960 in the *Coventry Standard*, had a similar experience. 'She had never heard my rather unusual Christian name before, and seized upon it for her very next book.' She went to the Christmas parties too, a different series, the *evening* ones.

'Good eve–ning! And how is your dear mo–ther?' was Angela's invariable greeting in the drawing-room as she shook hands with each girl in turn. Hunt the Thimble or General Post preceded supper, and the supper preceded crackers (the doctor wore a paper hat) and charades. 'Once,' wrote Noelle Osmond, 'when playing an American role, she came out with "Gee Whiz!" which, in her old-fashioned, slow utterance, made it very hard for me to keep a straight face.'

There were also the parties for the orphanage children, and one participant, Frances Saunt, not an orphan but the daughter of a member of the Natural History Society, remembers the glorious afternoon.

I think the highlight of our acquaintance was the new year of 1920 or 1921. The sisters gave a children's party at their home, 1 The Quadrant. Most of the guests were children from a local orphanage, but we were also invited. We were just an ordinary working-class family and nothing so exciting had ever happened to us before. Mother busily sewed new dresses for us, and when the great day arrived, off we went, by tramcar, across the town to The Quadrant. Cinderella arriving at the Palace couldn't have been more thrilled than we were to be entering such a big house! The door was opened by the maid and in we stepped, to be met in the hall by the sisters. Coats and hats were whisked away as we looked around in wonderment at the decorations. Although we didn't know the orphan children we were soon friends and had a wonderful time.

Before tea we all had turns on a swing which had been fixed for us in an archway in the hall, then we were all taken to the dining room, where the long table groaned under the weight of 'goodies'. There were sandwiches, jellies, blancmange and cakes – enough to feed an army it seemed – and to finish, everyone had trifle, specially laced with shiny silver threepenny pieces. I was lucky to find one in my helping, my sister was not so fortunate. We also had some beautiful Christmas crackers with lovely paper hats, not the kind of rubbish we get now, but properly shaped. Mine was a Dutch bonnet, and I treasured it for a long time afterwards.

After tea the fun really began. It seemed every few minutes, one or other of the sisters would say in a gently conspiratorial voice 'Now follow me, I have a little surprise for you'. We were led upstairs, downstairs, into first one room then another. In each one some fresh surprise awaited us. One room was crisscrossed with lines from which hung gaily wrapped parcels. Each of us was blindfolded and given a stick with which to find a parcel. I have forgotten what my gift was, but my sister recalls that hers was a toy cooking stove, complete with saucepans. In another room we all had to sit in the middle of the floor under a huge black umbrella. 'It's going to rain' said Miss Angela, and rain it did – a cloudburst of fruit bon-bons! You can imagine the wild scramble that followed. There were games of 'Blind Man's Buff', 'Tail on the Donkey', and many more which have now faded from memory.

At last came the sad moment when the party had to end. We were helped into our coats and as we left we each received an orange and a bag of sweets, and a farewell handshake from the two dear ladies who had given us such a wonderful treat. We talked of it long afterwards to our school friends. Today's children would no doubt think this kind of party extremely tame, but to us, in those days, it was something 'out of this world'.

The 'orphan' party was repeated in 1922, for in November Angela wrote to Marie Stopes (then Mrs Humphrey Roe) whom she had met in Polperro in Cornwall, and with whom she had an extended, intermittent correspondence:

A spinster lady can't do much in your line, but I love to 'mother' all the poor little forlorn children who are here, willy nilly, and don't find this planet a very bright place. Some of them are such dears, and so affectionate. I'm having a small orphanage of little derelicts to tea next week. They're rather pathetic small people – the flotsam of life! I'd like to take a few to Polperro sometime and try and get them strong. Otherwise they'll only carry on the same bad constitutions to another generation, alas!

While Angela catered for the girls (there was, *very* occasionally, a boy at a party) Walter saw to the moral well-being of his own sex by running a Crusader Class (a branch of the young people's Bible Class) for boys at the King Henry VIII School. Every year there was a 'birthday party' at the house, and Angela always cut the cake which, it was believed by the guests, she baked for the occasion. Sunday afternoon teas for the class were also regular events, with a conversational interval at five when the clock collection chimed out of synchronization. Amy and Angela made their appearances, poured tea from the silver tea service and passed the plates. Walter was greatly respected by the boys and the Crusader meetings and the tea parties were jolly occasions. He was not verbose, and his delivery (in a voice higher pitched than the average) was interesting and very much to the point. They might laugh behind his back at his small trilby hat with its pronounced indentation (it rested on the top of his head as if it were a size too small) but they revered his extensive knowledge, his little models of stationary steam engines (he was a remarkably able amateur engineer) and his kindness. He was, an ex-Crusader told me, 'very much a man'.

Parties of all kinds occurred in 'the works' but they are too numerous to mention. From 'coming-out' dances to beneficent gatherings of crippled children, they reflected Angela's passion for social jollity. There was never enough. She M.C.'d fund-raising whist drives for the Y.W.C.A., invariably wearing a black velvet jacket trimmed with white fur, and would cry out 'T–R–UMPS LADIES!' in her inimitable genteel voice. In her Cornish cottage, The Haven, she gave coffee evenings with competitions and pincushions as prizes. She organized picnics on the beach and in the moonlight, and at The Quadrant the musical evenings were notable (if not desirable) events. Arthur Birch, a pianist, attended at least two of these soirées.

At these functions, in company with other male guests, one deposited one's hat and coat in an ante-room, near the front entrance. (Where the ladies' powder-room was I have no notion.) I recall a white enamel ewer and basin standing in an iron frame in a corner of the cloakroom to enable us to wash our hands. After divesting ourselves of out-door trappings (and being warned beforehand to wear one's warmest winter woollies) one walked upstairs to the drawing-room which faced on to Greyfriars Green.

The room must have been a fair size, for I think it had double doors, [a trick of memory, there was only one door] which were opened wide as one's name was announced by a tidy maidservant in black with a white apron and cap. There was a coal fire in a grate in the side of the room facing the windows. This appeared to have been but recently lighted – hence the friendly warning about woollies from those in the know – and the night was freezing cold, with maybe an inch or two of snow lying on the ground.

With fresh arrivals, most probably knowing each other, conversation would begin, and after the ice had thawed a little, would become quite animated, and guests would move around. Miss Angela . . . spoke distinctly, precisely and slowly. I can still remember her saying with a smile 'I see Miss King is slowly circulating round the room'.

I recall my embarrassment at being asked to play a fairly elderly upright piano of uncertain vintage, [actually an Ibach which Walter bought just before the First World War] and finding when halfway through John Ireland's 'Island Spell' that the clocks were insisting on being heard.

About halfway through the evening we all trooped downstairs to the dining-room and sat for refreshment at a large rectangular or oval-ended table. It is possible that the catering may have been done by the Geisha Café, a rendezvous highly thought of by Coventry residents.

Noelle Osmond dreaded the formality of the musical evenings. Her sister, who played the violin, a cellist cousin and Noelle herself were sometimes invited (or was it summoned?) with older and more experienced musicians, including the cathedral organist. (Walter was a churchwarden, and arranged for the installation of the Carillon in 1927.) There were agonizing moments. The doctor insisted on turning the pages of the music, not always at the right time. Angela's applause was sometimes little more than a rebuke. One participant admitted secretly to wearing three vests in order to ward off the chill of The Quadrant drawing-room, and on a particularly bitter night even Amy quailed at the atmosphere; as the guests arrived she informed them that there were hot water bottles under the cushions on the chairs! It was Angela's children's parties – not unexpectedly – that were the pleasurable highlights. Adults received their invitations with a mixture of pride at the social attainment and sinking dread!

Angela had been given a leather-bound journal in 1906 in which she pasted newspaper clippings of an uplifting nature, concerning beauty, praise, heroism and the sunshine of life.

If our friends never made mistakes they would not need us as they do. If they never did wrong, they would probably be sufficient to themselves. Their very errors and blunders and wrongdoings are a claim upon our love and sympathy. To forgive and overlook and help is what friendship is for.

It was in this volume that she compiled her list of 'Virtues in my Friends to be copied and admired'. They included religious zeal, calm courage, patriotism, affection and a great capacity for love. She also inscribed 'A Heretic Hymn', the closest we ever come to her spontaneous feelings unencumbered by the necessities of plot.

When I am dead
Lord, do not send me to a dreary heaven
To spend eternities of idle days
In chanting forth the same continuous praise
Nay, let a lower planet to me be given
A place where I can work and try thro' strife
To fill some gap in thy great scheme of life
Giving my praise through service – this to me
The true and only blessedness would be
When I am dead.

Composed by A.B. and her true feeling!

Angela did not welcome idle moments. Indeed, her life between 1914 and 1939 was so full that one marvels at her energy. There was the Coventry Natural History and Scientific Society, the City Guild, the Y.W.C.A. (of which she became Vice-President in 1920 and President in 1928) and the Cathedral Committee work, which entailed poor visiting and of which she was a member between 1921 and 1925. There was also the travelling, which only ceased, perforce, during the war, during which period she frequently went on holiday in England. In her nature diary she records staying in the Cotswolds, at the White Hart Inn at Moreton-in-Marsh, and at the Lygon Arms at Broadway. There was the entertaining, the household shopping which she, and not Amy, undertook; at least one book a year and multifarious journalism; there were occasional broadcasts (in November 1925 she read her story, 'The Secret Supper'; in 1937 she took part in the Children's Hour *Roving Reporter* programme) and other activities relating to her professional life. She talked on 'The Modern Schoolgirl' at Harrods Literary Causerie on Friday, 6 November 1920 (tea in the Bookroom to follow), together with S. P. B. Mais, who spoke on 'The Art of Novel Writing'. She attended countless prize-givings, and visited other schools on Open Days and ordinary days. Vera Massey, then a pupil at Arley Castle School in Worcestershire, remembers Angela's arrival, and the girls' amusement at her fussy ensemble – all in shades of beige, with a cream 'ruff' and ruched coat and cream lace on the ornate hat. Angela, who was always on the look-out for spectacular hair, admired some particularly long pig-tails, and presumably acquired copy, as she always did. She also wrote an article on the school – perhaps at the request of the headmistress, Miss Edith Olive Johnson, described in the piece as a friend who had lately suffered a motor accident. Miss Johnson was striking, authoritative and enormously fat, with a mass of white hair, 'a face like an eiderdown', and a penchant for motoring, sometimes, according to Vera Massey, disappearing under the chassis to find a fault. She was a character who might have emerged from Angela's creative mind. Of the school, Angela, her style to the fore, wrote glowingly, but anonymously:

> It seems like a fairy-tale come true to gaze upon a real medieval castle in these days – standing on wide terraces and surrounded by what was once a treacherously deep moat, the castle of which I write, no longer houses noble knights and their retinue, but the 'fair ladyes' are there for it has of recent years become a boarding school for girls.

Day-girls and boarders wrote to Angela daily, sending her their photographs, and she always replied personally, often sending a photograph of herself in return. 'So pleased to know you aren't old and mouldy looking,' said one girl in pleased response. Some of the letters were deeply touching. Jean McCracken from Clydebank wrote twice.

> I would be very pleased if you could write down a list of books that you think good ones. I have never read Charles Dickens or Sir Walter Scott and I would like if you would write down the best ones, and I would get them. But I know there are some good books which, when one reads, they feel as if they could read them over again at any time and I hope I get some of them for my own.

Later, she elaborated.

> Dear Authoress, I am not a schoolgirl exactly, for I have left school. It has always been the dearest wish of my heart since I was a little girl to go to a boarding school. Unfortunately we are poor and I had just to go to a board-school. When I was about fourteen I was getting on well with my lessons and the headmaster told my parents I was clever and that they should send me to a higher grade school. But my parents had got the idea that schooldays should end when you are fourteen years of age so I had to leave just when I felt I could have stayed for years. I am awfully fond of reading and we have got a good public library in Clydebank and I read so many books my mother says she wonders I have any eyes left at all. I think I have the artistic sense because I am very fond of beautiful things and I love music. Unfortunately there is nobody to encourage it, because my parents seem to be the opposite of me in the extreme, even my sister (there is only two of us) and my friends don't understand me and say I am the quietest girl they ever saw. I suppose you will think this is a history of my life I am giving you. I don't know why I am telling you all this rigmarole, perhaps it is because I want a friend.

She found a friend in Angela, who preserved Jean's letters, but regrettably not her own replies. Girls poured out their longings and fantasies. Doris Stott, who always began 'Dear Angela', wrote: 'I am going to pretend I met you on a summers day. Here goes . . .' On another occasion (she was a regular correspondent) she said, 'I guess you will be surprised to receive another letter from me but I feel as if I want to write to you every day and tell you about things. Aren't "thoughts" nice things, I sometimes wonder whatever I should do if I could not think.'

'This is always my wish,' she said in yet another letter, 'to live in America, there would be four bungalows at the outskirts of a large wood. The house would be painted white and black, and there would be a river and we should always be boating, the sun would always shine and we should always be as bright and happy as the sun.'

Of all the letters she received, the one which made Angela most proud and which she mentioned in almost every interview she gave was from the Sharfunisa Begum of Hyderabad in January 1928. 'I was one of the lucky girls who got one of your nicest books as a prize,' wrote the Begum. 'The book was *The Leader of the Lower School* and I cannot tell you with what breathless interest I read it from cover to cover.'

The letter put Angela in a social quandary, because she did not know how to address such an elevated reader. She wrote to a friend in London, who gave her the information, adding: 'I am so glad to have your letter and to know that Indian girls are reading your books now.'*

Not only Indian girls, but Dutch, French, Polish, German, Scandinavian and American girls were reading Angela's books, the illustrative style changing radically from one country to another. Balliol Salmon's lovely elongated schoolgirls (he was Angela's favourite among her illustrators) were jettisoned for winsomeness in America and comic cartoons in France. *Une Ecole dans un manoir* does not hold a candle to *The Manor House School.*†

Angela did not employ an agent except for foreign rights, when she used Curtis Brown of Henrietta Street, London. She dealt with Mr Blackie himself, and he would make the journey to Coventry to discuss the next book with her. In spite of the intense literary activity, she did not neglect her painting, and in December 1925 she and Amy had an exhibition at the Walker Gallery in New Bond Street. 'We shall be at the Walker Gallery each morning from 11–12.30 while we are in town, so if you are anywhere near Bond Street from 1st–5th *do* come then, and we shall see you,' she wrote to Dr Marie Stopes.

Angela was fortunate that she lived at a time when maid-

* At the time of writing Blackie's have just been approached by a small Indian publishing firm to reprint, among other of Angela Brazil's books, *The Madcap of the School* and *The Secret of the Border Castle.*
† Illustrated by F. Moorsom.

servants were taken for granted. That she had the time to do so much was due to the smooth running of The Quadrant in her absence, as well as to her own organization. It is astonishing that she also had the time to cope with three complex and emotionally charged relationships, one of which directly involved a member of her estimable domestic staff.

[9]
FAITH AND CHARITY

The Quadrant maids, like all those employed by the committee of the Y.W.C.A. in Coventry, came from the Y.W.C.A. itself. Angela spoke at 'Sunday meetings' of girl members and at afternoon gatherings of the married members, and as she rose from the ordinary executive ranks to be the President, her visits became not unlike the descent of Lady Catherine de Burgh upon the Bennett household. Wednesdays the cooks, housemaids and parlourmaids went to the hostel in The Butts for a 'bit of company'. They were a race apart from the factory and shop workers who were in every night of the week. They were known as 'the Wednesday Girls'.

Annie* was a 'Wednesday Girl' and in 1917 she was also a domestic servant at Number One, The Quadrant. She was not local, having come to Coventry from Frome in Somerset where her family had a grocery business, and in Armistice year she became pregnant.

Angela, involved as she was with welfare, was able to help with arrangements for the confinement. She went, however, far beyond the assistance which an employer (particularly an employer who strictly observed all the proprieties of class and behaviour) might be expected to give. She organized the pre-natal care, and when the baby (a girl) was born in November 1918, she had her placed in the Hill Street Home, applied to the Courts for 'entire charge', allowed her to be fostered but not adopted, had her baptized at the cathedral with herself as one of the two godmothers, chose the baptismal name of Faith,* organized her education at the

* For reasons of privacy, these are not their real names.

St Agnes Convent of Charity in Bristol, and wrote regularly to her for twenty years. Why?

Faith, now a grandmother, was told by her foster-family that she was the illegitimate child of either Clarence or Walter Brazil. The welfare officer who handled the case, Miss Melrose, has not been traced, nor, in spite of considerable effort, has Annie or anyone who knew her. Official records (if there were any) were destroyed in the blitz, although I am certain that the father's name was left blank, as it was on the birth certificate. Angela made sure that she had covered the traces, but as always those matters uppermost in her mind worked their way into her books.

In general terms the theme of the foundling child had always fascinated her, so that it may be fortuitous that *A Gift From the Sea* was written soon after Faith's birth, and *A Fortunate Term*, with the fostered Bevis, published about twenty months afterwards. There is no possibility at all of mere coincidence with the one she was currently writing, *A Harum Scarum Schoolgirl*.

As the girls sat chatting, watching the ponies, and idly plucking flowers, they heard footsteps coming along the road, and presently a woman carrying a baby appeared round the corner. She was young and dark and gipsy-looking, and wore large ear-rings and a red cotton handkerchief knotted loosely round her brown throat. She stopped at the sight of Diana and Wendy and the ponies and seemed to consider for a moment. Then she walked boldly up to them, looked keenly in their faces and evidently chose Diana.

'Could you do me a kindness, Miss?' she asked. 'I've got to go up to the farm for a basket. I don't want to carry the baby with me; she's so heavy. If I leave her here on the grass would you keep an eye on her till I come back? I shan't be gone five minutes.'

Now Diana was fond of babies, and the little dark-eyed specimen, wrapped up in the plaid shawl, was pretty, attractive and fairly clean. For answer she held out her arms, received baby, shawl and feeding-bottle on her knee and constituted herself temporary nurse.

'She'll be good till I come back,' said the woman, turning up the lane that led to the farm.

The small person with the brown eyes was probably accustomed to be handed about. She did not jib at strangers, as might have been expected, but accepted the situation quite amiably.

Perhaps the vicinity of horses was familiar to her, and she felt at home. Diana, hugging her on her knee, freed her from the folds of the shawl and allowed her to kick happily. She was certainly a fascinating little mortal.

The chapter entitled 'Diana's Foundling' occurs after the one called 'Armistice Day'. The baby was never claimed, and, since bastardy was not a subject for schoolgirls, the mother was conveniently banished for being a criminal.

The poor little foundling, pending her mother's trial at the Assizes, was boarded out in the village with Mrs Jones, and Diana had permission to see her twice a week. Miss Todd communicated with the 'Home for Destitute Children', and received the reply that, should the mother be convicted, as seemed only too probable, they would be ready to receive the baby, and would apply to the judge for an order for entire charge, so that it should not be claimed and taken away to a possibly criminal life, when the mother's term of penal servitude was over.

And that, in terms of the plot, was that, an arbitrary introduction, tenuously linked, of the gipsy girl and her baby, who are then summarily dismissed. The book continued (as it had begun) with the friendship of spoilt Diana and sad Loveday. ('I'm falling in love with her,' she admitted to Wendy. 'I was taken with her, of course, the moment I saw her, but I believe now I'm going to have it badly. I think she's beautiful. If there were a peach competition, she'd win at a canter.') There were secret panels, false accusations, a stolen essay, and restored family fortunes, when orphan Loveday received her birthright.

Faith, needless to say, did *not* receive hers.

Just as Jackie Brazil was 'not a poor person's child and not exactly a gentleman's', so Angela – who was positively eighteenth century in her concept of the human chain – classified Faith, intending eventually that she should be her companion. She was probably surprised when the time came that Faith preferred marriage.

We have to consider the possibility, since there is no testimony, that Faith was the daughter of, say, a soldier who was killed at the front, or even of a male guest who stayed a day or two at The Quadrant (and the Brazils had many guests). If that was the case, would Angela have taken on the responsibility? Would she not have dismissed the servant and banished the friend, a friend no longer, or have helped the girl with the necessary medical and adoption matters, and left it at that? It seems, knowing what we do about her behaviour and character, that this is exactly what would have happened. Instead she made the child's upbringing her concern and no decisions were ever made without reference to her.

Faith's foster-mother had lost a child and was hoping for an adoptive substitute when she was told by Miss Melrose that there was a baby which would suit her well at the Hill Street Home. From the beginning it was made absolutely clear that there was no question of adoption at any time. Miss Melrose must have made her privy to the actual situation because Faith was eventually told the reason for Angela's close involvement.

She was sent by Angela to St Agnes's House of Charity to receive her education. Angela paid for all her needs, sent her presents and pocket-money, gave her a bicycle and a watch and visited her three times a year. Faith remembers being called out in class and introduced to a visitor as Angela Brazil's goddaughter, and this was how Angela signed her letters, and how Faith addressed her in her replies. From the age of seven she received letters regularly, with descriptions of the cottage in Wales, the holidays abroad and encouragement to be Christian and good. Among the memorable presents was a jointed doll in a big wooden box, with day clothes, night clothes and 'going out' clothes, a china head and long hair, and Faith was only allowed to play with it on special occasions. There were also copies of the first editions as they came out, and mementos from the travels: a leather purse from Rome, a model Swiss chalet; a brush and comb set; minia-ture cooking utensils, including scales. Angela had a coral necklace made for Faith when she was small, but, curiously, it was returned to her when Faith went to Bristol. She recalls a conversation with another child in which she both claimed and acknowledged Angela's contribution. During the Depression pocket money became scarce for most of the children.

'I bet my mother's got ten shillings,' boasted the friend.

'I bet my Godmother's got a pound,' said Faith, topping it.

'I bet she's got two pounds for what she sends you,' answered the other child, as a statement of fact.

Once Faith's schooldays were over she returned to Coventry, when she became engaged. Angela paid the deposit on the married couple's first house, and, together with Amy, bought the pram for the first baby and provided the entire layette. When Faith was having her second child, Angela paid for a resident nursery for the little boy. Later, via Angela, she fostered a child herself, but he turned out to be mentally deficient, and Dr Brazil described him as 'punch-drunk'.

'Don't keep this child, Faith,' he advised. Faith said the doctor always made her feel 'at home'.

Was he her father? Faith had been given to believe that it was Clarence. Since Jackie occasionally visited The Quadrant, and since Florence was never invited, it is feasible to assume that on occasions the socially fallen Clarence stayed there with his son. Faith gathered that for a time Clarence and Florence were separated, and that he went to South Africa. There is no way of finding out. He would have been sixty when Faith was born, but we know that although he married late in life he was capable of physical relationships with women. Without doubt a liaison with Annie would have been the *coup de grâce* as far as Angela was concerned! If anyone mentioned Clarence to her she 'closed up like a clam'. It would seem conclusive paternity in the circumstances, were it not for an extraordinary incident at that time which concerned Walter.

Outwardly Walter was rational, sedate and unimpassioned, but one night a member of the local clergy, a friend of his and a happily married man, was sitting at his dinner when there was a frantic knocking at the door. He opened it to find Walter in a distraught state, saying that although the hour was late he must have immediate advice. The rector ushered him in, whereupon Walter beseeched him for help. 'If I marry,' he asked wildly, 'would that contaminate my soul?' (An extraordinary query from a virulent and vitriolic anti-Roman Catholic.)

'Get out!' said the rector, who took it as a personal slur upon his own marital status. He assumed that Walter had a local woman in mind for life partnership, and that Angela's opposition had caused the man's distress. It seems possible that it was not *marriage* that Walter meant but his association with Annie. Amy and Angela were often away. Perhaps that had been the day when his years of repression had been overcome by desire. Certainly contemplation of marriage, at a time when the heyday of the blood is supposedly tame, is unlikely to have wrought such inner turmoil, such emotional havoc. ('Bloody prig!' said the rector later.) Meanwhile Faith, who may or may not be the only direct descendant of

Angelica and Clarence, follows her local football team, writes cogent letters to the local press and seemed to me to have the indomitable spirit and tireless energy of her godmother, Angela Brazil.

There was a second godmother, younger than Angela, who played a less prominent part in Faith's life, but a fundamental one in Angela's. Her name was Dorothy Milward, she was known as Dolly and was the daughter of Dr Harold Milward, a widower, colleague and friend of Walter's.* It has been suggested that both Walter and Angela had him in mind as her prospective husband, but if they did the plan came to nothing. It may have been these hopes that first prompted Angela's intense interest in Dolly, for in due course her love grew to be a possessive passion. In the 'List of Virtues found in my Friends' she wrote: 'Dorothy – Great capacity for love and enthusiasm.' She felt that this young, formative and eager mind was hers to mould, and the budding relationship, of great intellectual and emotional satisfaction to both of them, flowered into Angela's latest book, as arbitrarily placed in the overall plot and structure as the baby incident had been in *A Harum Scarum Schoolgirl*.

It seems that Angela began each book with only the barest plot outline or location setting, but that as she wrote her creative talent consumed life around her, fusing the fictional with the real. A ramble with the Coventry Natural History Society could produce Ingred's argument over the self-heal flower; a box of chocolates at her side in the Boudoir could give rise to an exclamation of delight in the dormitory; a 'soul friendship' could transform her heroine's world.

Lesbia Ferrars in *Loyal to the School* was, *au fond*, Angela herself recollected at fifteen, 'Celtic to the core' and loved by Regina 'much as a boy would, for her pretty hair, her dainty movements, and the general Celtic glamour that hung about her; she behaved, indeed, more like a youth in love than an ordinary schoolgirl chum'. In *For the School Colours* (which preceded it) we read of another Lesbia, deeply loved. Again it is a self-portrait, romanticized – Angela was incapable of honest personal appraisal – but what makes it particularly remarkable is that it is the only occasion when Angela wrote of herself as she was at the time; not as she had been as a child (in *A Terrible Tomboy*), not as she had been in the schoolroom (in *Loyal to the School*), but as a middle-aged, greying (albeit glamorously greying) woman. Of all the 'love affairs' in the forty-nine school stories written by Angela Brazil, that between

* For reasons of privacy, these are not their real names.

Avelyn Watson and Lesbia Carrington is the most riveting and the most revealing.

At the risk of being considered naïve, I would swear that the name Lesbia (*even* when linked with Regina) was chosen by Angela in innocence. I believe that, like other of her contemporaries, she found it a highly romantic name. Lesbia, after all, was the pseudonym used by Catullus to celebrate the lady he loved. Possibly the subconscious was at work, but not the conscious mind. The physical contacts and the physical admiration are sexual only to cynical and sophisticated contemporary readers. Homosexuality, paedophilia or whatever label our sexually oriented society might apply were beyond the reach of Angela's apprehension. It is relevant to point out that *The Well of Loneliness*, Radclyffe Hall's study of female homosexuality, was not published until 1928, when Angela was fifty-nine. In any case, even if she had read it, Angela considered herself intensely feminine (of the two, Amy was the more masculine in appearance and dress, wearing trilby hats not unlike Walter's); while acknowledging intense feelings between girls and women, she knew them only as romantic friendships, customary and acceptable between Victorian women. Angela understood the emotions, and portrayed them with immense sympathy. She did not attempt to understand the causes and it could not have occurred to her to do so. The 1960s produced Regina Outre-Mer and Miss Mount* but Regina Webster and Miss Pratt† emerged not only from an earlier decade but from a psychologically different era. The forty years between the two books makes them as remote from one another as a David Hockney and a Burne-Jones.

Lord Berners amused his effete London circle in 1936 by lampooning his friends in his privately published satire, *The Girls of Radcliff Hall by Adela Quebec*: Daisy in her black rubber mac, Miss MacRogers with her 'very nice cottage-bungalow in the Lake District called Balmoral', Cecily 'as clever with her paint-brush as she was with her needle' and simply stunning in charades, and Miss Carfax who liked to 'form young people'. His accurate stylistic mimicry‡ gave odd testimony to Angela's extraordinarily wide

* In Brigid Brophy's witty novella *The Finishing Touch*.
† In Angela Brazil's deadly serious *Loyal to the School*.
‡ 'It was a merry scene, all these fresh young faces glowing in the firelight; a scene that Raphael or Botticelli would have loved to paint.'
'Miss Carfax sat alone before a dying fire. Memories grave and gay fluttered like autumn leaves across her brain.'

success, and provided the Blakean dividing line between Innocence and Experience. For the first time she became a different kind of cult figure; her first editions are now collected on both sides of the Atlantic for reasons which would have been totally foreign to her as she sought to pass on the schoolgirl ethic first learned at her estimable mother's knee.

Lesbia Carrington (in *For the School Colours*) was a 'poetess', and she wore mauve. Angela Brazil wore mauve most of the time too. This would be a superficial identity link were it not for other internal evidence, and the friendship of Dolly Milward, who, one may reasonably assume (although without certainty), was Avelyn Watson.

It was Easter time when the Lavender Lady first rose upon the horizon of Lyngates. She came with the dog violets and the ground ivy and the meadow orchises, and several other lovely purple things, at least that was how her advent was always associated in Avelyn's mind. She took the furnished bungalow near the church, lately vacated by the curate, and it was rumoured in the village that she composed music and had published poetry, and that she had come down to the country for a rest.

When Avelyn first saw her she was sitting in the flowery little garden raised above the road. She wore a soft lavender dress and an old lace fichu, and she had dark eyes and eyebrows, and cheeks as pink as the China roses, and fluffy grey-white hair that gleamed like a dove's wing as the sun shone on it. She looked such a picture as she sat there, all unconscious of spectators, against a background of golden wallflowers and violet aubrietias, that Avelyn was obliged just to stand still and gaze. In that thirty seconds she fell in love with the Lavender Lady. It was not a mere mild liking, but a sudden, romantic, absolute, headlong falling in love. It had come all in a minute and overwhelmed her. She crept away softly to dream dreams about the vision she had seen in the garden. At home there were some beautiful illustrated editions of William Morris's *Earthly Paradise* and of Dante Gabriel Rossetti's poems. She took them out and pored over them. The gorgeous pre-Raphaelite pictures had always appealed to her innate artistic sense, and set her nerves athrill with a something she could not analyse. There was not one of them so beautiful as the Lavender Lady among the flowers.

'She's a little like "The Blessed Damozel",* who leaned out "from the gold bar of heaven",' mused Avelyn. 'And then again she's like Gainsborough's picture of "The Duchess of Devonshire". I wonder what her name is, and if I shall ever know her? I don't believe I'd dare speak to her. I'd be too shy.'

For a whole week Avelyn, terribly in love, lived in a mystic world in which the Lavender Lady, robed in the glory of the purple night and stars, was as the central sun, and she herself revolved like a planet round her orbit. The family could not understand why she insisted upon choosing heliotrope for her new dress.

That was the beginning. Avelyn walked past the cottage every evening and once threw a bunch of violets over the wall, then ran away, frightened at her own daring. At the sight of the Lavender Lady (in black and white this time, 'with a bunch of violets and a big picture hat trimmed with silver ribbon, and a white ostrich boa and dainty white kid gloves') in church, Avelyn's heart 'gave a great thump'. When the verger showed her to a seat in the next pew but one, 'Avelyn felt thrills running down her spine'.

Her joy and apprehension knew no bounds when Mother decided to call, and sister Daphne preferred the company of Captain Harper, thus resigning 'her privilege, as elder daughter, to call on the Lavender Lady'. Outwardly self-possessed, but inwardly agitated, Avelyn entered the Lavender Lady's domain, and at this point Angela Brazil set down her credo, her hopes and her dreams.

The half-hour's visit passed like a dream.

'You'll come and see me again, dear, won't you?' said Miss Carrington, as she held Avelyn's hand in goodbye. The hot colour flooded the girl's face. Her eyes shone like stars.

'Oh, may I?' she cried impulsively.

That afternoon marked an epoch. Friendship is a matter more of temperament than of years. That the Lavender Lady was middle-aged and Avelyn barely sixteen, made not the slightest difference to either of them. Each character dovetailed comfortably into the other. Miss Carrington had a great sympathy for girls, and she seemed to understand Avelyn at once. As for the latter, she had utterly lost her heart. But for the fear of

* This is how Regina described Lesbia Ferrars in the chapter called 'The Blessed Damozel' in *Loyal to the School*.

making herself a nuisance she would have nearly lived at the
bungalow. She went there very often by special invitation, and
spent glorious, delightful afternoons sitting in the garden,
talking about art and books and music, and the foreign places
Miss Carrington had visited. It fascinated Avelyn to hear about
Venice and Rome and Sicily and Egypt, and made her long to go
and see them for herself.

'You shall, some day, when the war's over,' said the Lavender
Lady confidently.

(After the war and over the years Avelyn–Dolly did accompany
Angela on her travels abroad.)

To Avelyn it was a most inspiring friendship, that roused
dormant hopes and ideals in her nature which promised to make
rapid growth afterwards. Her Lavender Lady proved to be the
most delightful of confidants. It was possible to tell her everything. She never laughed at Avelyn's secrets, though she was
merry enough on occasion.

The substance of the book was the amalgamation of a boarding-
school and a day-school, with Avelyn, a weekly-boarder, 'neither
fish, flesh, fowl nor good red herring!' It was the Lavender Lady,
stroking her hair and holding her hand, with a mixture of urgent
exhortation and sympathy, who found the solution. Thus
spiritually armed Avelyn returned to school with the strength to
form a 'Loyal to the School Club' and to propose the combination
of the school colours.

It is significant that in Angela's next novel, *Head Girl at the
Gables*, written immediately afterwards (Blackie's received the
manuscript of *For the School Colours* on 25 February 1918 and
that of *Head Girl at the Gables* on 21 October the same year) the
Lavender Lady appears again as amanuensis in the guise of artist
Margaret Lindsay.

She was one of those people who seem neither old nor young
for her intense personality quite overmastered any ravages time
might have made in her appearance . . . she proved a veritable
fairy godmother, not in painting alone, but in other matters as
well. Lorraine had reached that stage of girlhood when she
badly needed a new impulse and a different mental atmosphere.
It is so difficult sometimes for parents to realize that their

children are growing up, and require treating from a revised standpoint. Unconsciously and out of sheer custom, they rule them *de haut en bas*, and then wonder why the little confidences of budding womanhood are given instead to sisters or friends.

Though she was old enough in some ways, in others Miss Lindsay was that most delightful of persons, 'a chronic child'.

(Miss Lindsay, who specialized in painting fairies, owed her art to Amy's American friend, Hildegarde Cooke.)

Dolly had no mother, and Angela, receiving a response as warm as Avelyn's and Lorraine's, took it upon herself to provide the 'different mental atmosphere' in a role of teacher–parent–friend.

Dolly did not marry. Once she and a young man, mutual friends of the Brazils, decided they were in love, and went to The Quadrant to tell Angela the news. She took it calmly, asked if they had bought the engagement ring and, on discovering that they had not, said that it must be her present to them. She pressed some money into the young man's hand, and it wasn't until they were on their way to the jeweller's that he looked to see the extent of her generosity, and discovered that she had given him a ludicrously small sum that would have bought a ring in Woolworth's but nowhere else. Her calculated mockery was as crushing and final as any classroom diatribe; the boy was miserably humiliated and no doubt Dolly was later told what a ridiculous game it had all been.

Dorothy Milward attended Faith's baptism at the Old Cathedral with Angela. She took her responsibility seriously, and visited Faith in Bristol on separate occasions from Angela, so that Faith had a double quantity of visits. Physically Dolly was small and plump, with the kind of appearance which scarcely alters over the years. In photographs she is instantly recognizable at sixteen and forty. She had an unchanging hair-style and a pleasant, cheerful, friendly expression, which, Faith said, was true to character. She found her easy-going on those school outings; they went into Lyons Corner teashop and Faith was told to pick anything she wanted. She always chose the biggest cream cake.

Dolly often stayed at The Quadrant, and at Ffynnonbedr until it was sold in the 1920s to a member of Leila's family. She was generally with Angela at The Haven in Polperro on her several visits a year. Faith last heard from her from St Albans in 1945 when her son was born. In 1947 Amy made her last will and testament, leaving Dorothy pictures painted by herself and by

Angela, giving the address then as Westgate-on-Sea. My letters in the local press asking for information met with no response, neither did appeals in the personal column of *The Times* and to the Y.W.C.A., for which Dolly worked in St Albans (the branch is no longer in existence). It was in 1947 that Angela herself died. There is no further reference.

Angela's were jealous friendships, and those who transgressed were not forgiven. A. Morris-Gilbert was enmeshed in the tentacles of the household at The Quadrant and was driven by the pressures to the edge of destruction. Angela liked to hold the reins; with Faith there was no problem, and with Dolly few fears, but the highly sensitive schoolboy, taken to the house by his father in 1912, was less malleable and meeting the Brazils profoundly affected his life.

Gilbert Morris was a 'child prodigy'. He made his first public appearance at the Society of Artists concerts in Birmingham at the age of six, having been taught from the time he was two and a half by his father, Albert Edward Morris, who had himself been a concert pianist in America. For some reason Gilbert never knew, when his father returned to England he gave up playing and went into the piano business instead; it was in 1912 that Walter Brazil entered the showrooms of Dale, Forty and Company, piano merchants, and consulted Mr Morris about the purchase of a piano for his recently acquired house at The Quadrant.

It was on these premises that Walter heard Gilbert play, and, greatly impressed, he asked Mr Morris to bring his son to the house to perform for Angela. Mrs Morris, in the meantime, had been taken ill. Walter was sent for, diagnosed appendicitis and sent her to hospital, where she was successfully operated on. From then on Walter was the Morris family doctor.

Gilbert remembers how, on his first visit to The Quadrant, he was received with great formality and kindness. He was probably fed with cakes and chocolates, bearing in mind Angela's aptitude for giving children the foods she liked best.

Angela had always believed, as we know, in the fostering of talent in the young, and it must have been an exciting decision when she and Walter decided to become the patrons of the gifted Gilbert. If there was an element of patronization in the patronage he was too young to know it. Indeed, he valued their friendship, and gradually he became part of the *ménage*, dropping in at the house whenever he was passing and often staying the night. He felt it was his 'second home', and he had no idea at that time that there was what Walter called 'the fund', and that he was in a sense repaying them when he played (as became customary) at their parties.

'So many people want to hear you play,' Angela would say, and he never thought of querying the implicit command.

During the war, the Brazils took a great interest in musical Belgian refugees, including a string quartet. Gilbert gave a recital in aid of the Refugee Fund, and lived what amounted to a professional life, playing at functions and musical events at weekends, in the evenings and on holidays while coping with the normal demands of school. He was not yet fifteen.

The dedication needed in any musical training was stressed in a number of Angela's books, and all of them derive directly or indirectly from Gilbert. *The Girls of St Cyprian's*, written early in 1914 when his future seemed as personal a possession of the Brazils as any of the doctor's clocks, indicates the encouragement and the hopes she and Walter cherished, the conversations they must have had with each other, with Gilbert's parents and with the boy himself. They were blissfully unaware of the strain that was beginning to affect him as they steamrollered him towards the career that would bathe them, they believed, in reflected glory.

Completely unknown to Gilbert, they made plans for him to attend the Royal College of Music, and Angela wrote the necessary letter of recommendation. Having done that much, true to her particular code of behaviour she felt she had 'done her bit' and gave the letter to Gilbert to post. He failed to do it. Whether or not he simply forgot he had it in his pocket or whether the motives had a far deeper psychological basis it is impossible to say, but Angela may have understood him more than he realized. When Claudia did exactly the same thing in *Head Girl at The Gables*, 'there was a curious shade of relief mingled with her contrition'. The authorities naturally complained, but the authoress implied that her sympathy was with the recalcitrant pupil. 'It's really too bad!' said Miss Janet Kingsley, headmistress of The Gables. 'You've ruined your own career, and no-one but yourself to thank for it! Why, the scholarship was as good as gained!'

'I feel that a girl who could forget such an immensely important step in her own career, would be of no use to us,' (wrote the principal of the college Claudia had been destined to attend).

But, confided Claudia to Lorraine:

'I can't tell you how relieved I am really . . . I never wanted to go and that's a fact.'

'Claudia!' began Lorraine, with sudden enlightenment, 'were you going to be *home-sick*?'

Gilbert had to leave home nevertheless, but he was within bicycling distance. He went as a day-boy to Rugby School, living in digs, and, as before, the professional work continued in every moment of his free time. It was arranged by Walter and his father, and he just did as he was told.

In 1917 he made a tour of the Midlands. He had not been consulted. It was a matter of being informed. ('You play in West Bromwich on Wednesday.') About that time, cycling over from Rugby one afternoon, he was told with some ceremony by Angela that she and Walter intended to make him their heir. Artists usually had a 'beastly struggle' to make their way in the world, she said, but they were going to see that it did not happen to Gilbert. He was flattered and puzzled, but the seemingly altruistic gesture was soon explained. Walter approached Mr Morris and confidently offered to adopt Gilbert, on the proviso, of course, that he took the name Brazil! The amazed parents refused but were persuaded to ask Gilbert himself and he too made a flat rejection. It was not a decision which pleased the Brazils but they managed to discount the setback. When I began my research for this book, several people wrote to me from Polperro, mentioning 'an adopted son' and giving Gilbert's real and professional names. Embarked on a course, Angela had simply discounted opposition. She had no intention of allowing the technicality of a legal stamp to obtrude upon her decisions – but there was a hidden resentment just the same.

One morning Gilbert was missing at Rugby School. Someone was sent to his lodgings but he was not there and in due course a search party set out. He was found hours later sitting on a canal bank in a catatonic state. He was taken home to Coventry, and Walter, always concerned and humane, decreed that he should never return to school.

It did not occur to him that he and Angela were in any way responsible for the breakdown.

Gilbert rested and recovered, although he endured occasional bad migraines. In her journal 'Living Your Best' Angela copied out an essay he had written for her in 1917. It was called 'Music and Its Relation to Human Nature'.

He became music master at Coventry Preparatory School, and took private pupils, building up a good practice. It was then that the Brazils decided to send him to Paris to study with Lazare Lévy, a renowned teacher who in 1920 had taken over from Cortot as principal of the Conservatoire. It was arranged that he should accompany Amy, who had planned a period at an art studio, and her goddaughter, Leila's daughter, Carol Samuels.

Carol was an aspiring and talented artist. She had already spent a memorable holiday abroad with Amy, who believed that a god-parent should do more than teach the catechism. She had done that, with gentle insistence, when Carol was small. She considered travel to be essential to the education of the modern girl. Angela, in more than one book, described it as 'the coping stone'.

They had, on that occasion, gone to Italy. Angela had arranged with Mr Blackie that her new book should encompass a visit to Vesuvius, and for part of the time she accompanied Carol and Amy on their tour. They travelled by wagon-lit to Paris, from there to Venice and Florence, where they stayed near the Ponte Vecchio, then to the Bay of Naples, Sorrento and, of course, Vesuvius. When Angela was with them they lived in the best hotels, but when she returned to England to write *The School in the South* they moved into a pension. When they made the breakfast tea, Amy put the pot to one side and added water to the tea-leaves later in the day. Angela (and Mr Blackie) held the purse strings; there were limits to her generosity when she was not there to enjoy the fruits.

In Paris Angela again stayed in a first-class hotel – she was researching this time for *Schoolgirl Kitty* – but Amy, Carol and Gilbert moved into the Villa des Dames in the Rue Notre Dame des Champs, which had once been the residence of the ladies of the Luxembourg court. There were about forty-five students of the various arts there, including an American artist, Grover Weaver, and Simon Elwes, who was with his mother and sister. Amy and Carol shared a room, and Gilbert joined them for breakfast, which they prepared themselves. Afterwards Amy and Carol went off to their *atelier*, and Gilbert practised until it was time to meet again for lunch. Angela and Walter paid his expenses but they were all on a limited budget and the meal usually consisted of scrambled eggs and cheese. In the evenings, unless Angela was with them, they ate at the International Students' building on the Boulevard Mich, where Gilbert would play for long periods in the music room. Whenever they could afford it they went to concerts. They heard, among others, Mark Hambourg, Busoni and Petri.

For the two young people it was life-enhancing. They were devoted to Amy. They felt they were at the very centre of creative activity; Gilbert received nothing but praise from his teacher and Carol, restricted at home by time and space, enjoyed artistic freedom for the first time. They thought they were on the brink of a productive and fulfilling future, but in retrospect Carol felt that, in giving so much but so little, the Brazils had been both kind and cruel. The door opened, and then closed with a bang. At the end of six months they all went home to England. Carol had not expected an extension because from the beginning she had known that Amy could not afford more, but Gilbert had been led to believe he was to have a full year in Paris, followed by six months' break and then a second year. Suddenly, at the end of Amy and Carol's stay, he was instructed to return with them.

'I'm afraid,' said Walter, 'there's no more money in the fund.' It was the first time that Gilbert had heard of 'the fund' and he was shocked and horrified. He believes now that if the preliminaries had not been so far advanced, he would not have gone at all. For reasons he has never understood, Angela pulled out the rug.

[10]
FAIRY GODMOTHER

Angela bought her cottage in Polperro soon after the First World War. It was by no means picturesque, being Victorian and semi-detached, but it was covered with ivy and set halfway up a cliff overlooking the harbour, and the view was dazzling. She referred to it in Coventry as 'my estate in Cornwall'. It had, at first, no proper plumbing, and a local boy, Dick Joliffe, carried water up the steep steps for a penny a can. Cornwall and Devonshire became, with increasing frequency, the background for the books. Chagmouth in *A Fortunate Term* was Polperro itself.

As always, Angela was active and involved. Polperro provided her with new and interesting friends; there were apparently several meetings with Sir Hugh Walpole, with Sir Arthur Quiller-Couch and with Dr Marie Stopes, who had built a sort of shelter-cum-camp at Coomb Beach. It was Angela who made the first overtures. 'We both publish through Messrs Blackie and Son,' she wrote on 22 May 1922,

and I have your book on Fossil Plants at home and appreciate it greatly. I also have a country cottage at Polperro where I run away from the 'madding crowd'. I don't want to suggest anything so conventional as 'calling', but it would give me great pleasure to meet you, and if anytime you are shopping or posting letters in Polperro I shall be delighted if you look me up. My wee house is up a flight of steps on the Chapel Rock.

They met, and liked one another. In June Angela wrote: 'I shall be down again in August, also Dr B., and our young musician Gilbert, and a girl violinist friend who plays very well.' She followed it up with an invitation to Marie Stopes and her husband, Humphrey Roe:

> Dr and Miss Brazil
> request the pleasure of the company of
> Mr and Mrs Humphrey Roe and friends at a
> *Private Concert*
> to be held on Friday, August 1st, at 8.15 p.m.
> at The Hut, The Coombs.
> Mr Morris-Gilbert (pupil of M. Lazare Lévy, Paris)
> will give a piano recital, and other friends have
> kindly promised to assist.

Thus to their friends Walter and Angela gave the impression that they were still Gilbert's prime supporters. In fact they had not only severed him from his studies in Paris but had stepped between him and opportunity with a shattering disregard for his personal feelings and for everything they themselves had done for him.

M. Lazare Lévy regarded Gilbert as a brilliant pupil, and was unhappy at the harsh curtailment of his time in Paris; perhaps because of it he went to some lengths to arrange a recital tour for Gilbert in the United States; there was only one condition, that the first concert should be underwritten, but there was little chance that it would not be a success.

Gilbert did not have this kind of personal money, but in those days everything depended on it, as Angela had pointed out on the occasion when she had announced that he was to be her heir. Scholarships, foundations and bursaries now obviate the need for private patronage, but Gilbert was born too early. Naturally he approached the Brazils to be his guarantors, and unnaturally they refused. Instead they invited him to Polperro, arranged a small concert to show off the results of his six months in Paris and Angela wrote some songs for him to set to music.* 'There seems an absolute wicked fate against my saying "Goodbye"!' she wrote to Marie Stopes, as the summer drew to a close.

I was sorry not to see you when you called and wished Dolly had told me you were there, for I was only resting upstairs. I wanted to come to Lizzen today but yesterday I had promised to

* *My Posy and Other Songs, Sweetheart of Yesterday,* New World Publishing Company.

take a large party of young folk for a birthday picnic, and of course the rain made it impossible, so I took them all today instead, and we are only just home. Tomorrow I shall be busy getting the Haven ready for shutting up, and putting everything in order to leave on Saturday morning. If you should chance to be in Polperro on Friday will you call and see me? If not I hope we shall meet next time we are both here again. It has been nice to see you this summer, and I wish you were nearer and could have come to the dances. My sister and I are going to Brittany next Tuesday. We have booked passages on the White Star Liner 'Majestic' to Cherbourg, so it ought to be a swift crossing, and we shall come back via Paris and Dover. I don't fancy the twelve hour passage to St Malo! Mr Gilbert's 1st Volume of songs is to be published in October, so he is very excited. He will have to join the Society of Authors etc. when he can show some publications of his own! I hope your work will have a very successful winter season. I shall look out for your name in the newspapers now! With kindest remembrances and thanks for all your hospitality,

Sincerely yours,
Angela Brazil.

Gilbert and Carol might have found the Paris experience less than satisfactory but it had been admirable for Angela's purposes. As Clifford and Kitty Carrington (surnames tended to occur more than once in the Works and Carrington was a particular favourite) they were a pair of art students staying together with musical sister Gwenda at the 'Maison Verte' in *Schoolgirl Kitty*. Auntie Vi, who accompanied them and studied painting too, was Amy, and the 'Maison Verte', described in detail, was a reproduction of the Villa des Dames, even to its location overlooking the Luxembourg Palace.

Every outing, incident and entertainment (there is even a concert by Mark Hambourg) gave the book bulk,* and the trip to Brittany mentioned by Angela to Marie Stopes provided three additional chapters, 'Adventures in Brittany', 'A Sketching Party' and 'Round the Wood Fire', as well as the pleasant autumn excursion for Angela and Amy. Earlier in the story 'A Moonlight Picnic' in Cornwall, with a bonfire, games, fireworks and glow-worms, gave Mr Blackie an expenses-free chapter as a bonus!

* The English edition was 317 pages.

Gilbert's setbacks were not over. Seven or eight months after he came back to England, he was knocked off his bicycle by a car and his right hand hideously torn. The wound became septic and it was nine months before he was able to play again. Angela arranged for him to stay in Polperro in a studio which contained a Steinway Grand. Walter gave him a small car and gradually his life established itself again. He became involved in the musical activities of the south-west, did some broadcasting, gave recitals, and took private pupils, among them Constance Perry, who had come to Polperro with her mother and who later became his wife.

The final dispute with the Brazils occurred over Gilbert's first London recital at the Grotrian Hall in 1927. Angela had had nothing to do with the arrangements, but she immediately claimed the occasion as a personal achievement. 'I am sending you a notice of this recital by Gilbert,' she wrote to Marie Stopes on 21 September,

> and hope you may be able to go. He has improved immensely in technique and his own compositions are beautiful, especially the pieces, which somehow convey the sound of the *Cornish* water on the rocks.
>
> The Manager of the Grotrian Hall thinks very highly of him, and I hear many Musical Critics are to be at the concert. We are all going to hear him. I am just back from Polperro, and had a lovely holiday there.
>
> I hope you are well, and dear little Buffkins thriving.
>
> With love, yours affectionately, Angela.

(Buffkins was the Humphrey Roes' child.)

Three days later, having received a conditional acceptance, Angela wrote again:

> How delightful if you can come to G's recital. Dr B and my sister and I shall be there, and we should *love* to meet you. Dr B says 'Oh *do* tell her to be sure and come!' We would all go to the green room afterwards so that you could meet Gilbert again, and then all have tea together if you will be our guest. Dolly Milward will be with us – she met you once at Polperro and admires you immensely – also Gilbert's fiancée, Miss Perry (such a nice girl, and an absolute sheet anchor to him, does all his secretarial work and has a calm business head!) so we should be such a jolly little party together.

The party was not jolly. The day, which should have been pleasurable, became unbelievably fraught. Gilbert had not been told of Angela's plans, nor had he been informed by his parents that they, too, had planned tea with friends. Gilbert was subject to nosebleeds, and to his horror one began before the recital and he played in utter misery, terrified that it would start again in the middle. Afterwards, with reporters trying to interview him, there was a scene with Angela, who was enraged that he contemplated abandoning her for his parents. She commanded: 'You're coming with us!'

Gilbert divided his time, but the tea at Marshall and Snell-grove's was not the celebration Angela had intended. From then on the relationship cooled. They continued to write, and met occasionally, always in a friendly atmosphere, but Gilbert was aware of the unspoken disapproval and disappointment. In 1932 he moved to London, and became for a time Musical Editor of the Amalgamated Press.

'Look, old chap,' Walter had once said to him, 'even if you don't feel any of it, walk onto that platform as if you owned the earth.' The platforms upon which Gilbert chose to walk became fewer. He had lost heart.

In 1937 he went to Coventry to give a short recital at a reception at the Y.W.C.A., during the National 'Blue Triangle' week. It was a favour to Angela, and the local press praised the compositions of 'the well-known pianist and composer, Mr Morris-Gilbert', but it was a long way from the American concert halls and the hopes of M. Lazare Lévy. It would be interesting to know if Angela ever had a moment's compunction. More likely she thought that it was Gilbert who had let her down.

The most bizarre literary request of the twentieth century must have been when Marie Stopes approached Angela Brazil to allow her to adapt one of her school stories for the stage. The sad part of it was that Angela gently refused.

Marie had been staying at The Quadrant, during which time she had addressed a meeting in Coventry. One imagines her making the suggestion in the Boudoir after dinner, having perhaps eaten venison, a meat stocked by Angela's butcher in Hertford Street and of which the Brazils were fond, and cooked fresh, like lamb. They might have been enjoying chocolates, or smoking the Reske Minor cigarettes which Walter insisted Angela used for her 'nerves', and which she held in one of those pincer-ring holders.

Dr Stopes could even have been sipping sloe gin, which the Brazils, teetotal themselves, made and served in the twenties and thirties. ('We pick our own sloes in Cornwall,' Angela would annunciate to her guests.) Walter, one of his patients said gratefully, never tried to put a man off his drink.

Marie Stopes enjoyed her visit and wrote to Angela, thanking her. Angela, who had been reflecting on the possibility of stage adaption, replied in a letter marked 'Private', and it is the only extant document in which she assessed her own work.

'Dear Dr Marie Stopes,' she wrote, and although the letter is undated, the mode of address and the content place it clearly in the early stages of their friendship, possibly in the winter of 1922–3:

I am so glad you had a good journey, and only hope you are not too tired after your visit to Coventry. It was a great pleasure to have you with us, and we thoroughly enjoyed your company. I am sending you a copy of the Coventry Herald which has a good report of your meeting, and I also return your pretty scarf, which was left in a drawer.

I have been looking over my books, but really I am afraid there is not one which meets the exact requirements. They were not written with any idea of adaption for the stage, and I have always tried to cram in outdoors adventures to suit the taste of my young readers. They would be admirable for the films, but on the stage it would be quite impossible to render such scenes as walking on the roof of a manor house, getting lost in the mist, overtaken by the tide, or games of hockey and tennis tournaments or bicycling or other mad escapades in which the heroines indulge. The whole gist of the plot in all the books depends practically on what one would call 'large action', and could not be confined to one or two scenes. Another point is that the particular charm of my books is supposed to lie in the writing, the way I describe scenes etc., and this of course, could not be reproduced in dialogue, any more than essays could be dramatized.

It is most kind of you to propose such a plan, but I don't believe there is a single one of the books that you could use for the purpose with any chance of success. I shall hope to come and see your fairy tale when it is produced. I am sure it will be lovely. How enterprising you are!

With kindest remembrances,
Affectionately yours,
Angela Brazil.

Angela had, as we know, written fairy plays herself, but they concerned a different species of fairy from the ones which were increasingly fascinating her. Her plays showed the influence of the brothers Grimm, but she had always nurtured a hankering belief in the more ethereal sprites. She wrote in *My Own Schooldays*:

I had only one little adventure on the borders of the psychic world, and it still seems so absurd and unaccountable that I hesitate to chronicle it. Yet here it is, just as it happened. I was six or seven years old at the time, and I was running upstairs to the playroom in the attic. As I reached the corner of the last flight, there, beside the bannisters, stood a wee man about three feet high, with a plum-pudding for a head, and almonds for eyes, nose and mouth, exactly like a Christmas card. I looked at him as a collector would view a new species of moth, with deepest interest, then turned, ran downstairs again and told the thrilling news to my mother. She went on sewing with the utmost calm.

'Go upstairs again and he'll probably be gone!' she replied.

So I went – and he *was* gone! But I am still wondering! *What* did I see? He was apparently quite as real and substantial as the bannisters, or as my mother, or any other solid fact of nature. Why, oh why, if I was to be vouchsafed a glimpse of a faerie creature, need it have a plum-pudding head? I was no glutton; I was not even very fond of plum-pudding, and would so infinitely have preferred the bluebell variety of sprite. I gave it up then – and I give it up now.

There had been analogous references in the early books, and many references to fairy and faerie – palaces, grottoes, dells and, indeed, moments. Cornwall, with its folklore and superstitions, awakened her dormant credulity. Miss Lindsay, the artist in *Head Girl at The Gables* – based on Hildegarde Cooke whose landscapes and seascapes revealed hundreds of elfin creatures among the leaves or under the crests of the waves – explained to Claudia how she would paint her as Kilmeny from *At the Back of the North Wind*.

'Well, you see, I'm going to paint you just coming home, in the evening glow with the yellow light behind, and the thistles and brown bracken. The sheaf of golden ragwort will be like a wand, and you'll still have the spell of fairyland in your face. I'm not sure if I shan't put in a few half-transparent fairies escorting you back; they'd blend among the thistledown.'

In *The Little Green School*, the most 'Cornish' of all the novels, she recounted tales of the piskies with a semi-seriousness that took her readers one step further beyond Miss Lindsay's imaginative work. 'The piskies dance here on moonlit nights. Betsey said she saw them once, and they had little red cloaks on.' Stories she heard from Polperro residents – this book is notable for its use of Polperro family surnames such as Joliffe (the boy who brought water to her cottage) and Giles (her grocer) – were integrated into the narrative.

In 1920 Angela read Sir Arthur Doyle's article 'Fairies Photographed' in the *Strand Magazine*, in which he questioned but ultimately supported the photographic evidence. In 1921 he wrote a second piece, 'The Evidence for Fairies', with further illustrations, including 'Iris, with Fairy Carrying a Bunch of Harebells', carrying the caption: 'The fairy is standing almost still, poised on the bush-leaves. The wings were shot with yellow; upper part of dress very pale pink.'

Angela removed the pages and made a special folder of cardboard on which she stuck cut-outs of fairies and flowers, keeping it with other special papers in her Boudoir. Among them was the tourists' hand-out history of Joan the Wad, Queen of the Lucky Cornish Piskies. This reprinted a poem by local resident Arthur Quiller-Couch on the pisky origins,

> We were not good enough for heaven,
> Nor bad enough for hell;
> And therefore unto us 'twas given
> Unseen on earth to dwell

to which was added a verse by another hand:

> We're sometimes high and sometimes low
> And Sometimes in the Sod,
> And if you want luck well enow
> Then keep near 'Joan the Wad'.

She talked a great deal about 'faery lore, pixies and hobgoblins, whilst looking starry-eyed', said Gilbert Morris, discussing the many facets of Angela's character. Irene Straker, one of the Y.W.C.A. girls, went with Angela in 1939 on a short holiday to Stratford where they stayed at the New Place Hotel. 'We would take a bus and cut lunch and go off into the country and walk from one village to another, sometimes across the fields, and sometimes along the country lanes. I heard Cornish tales of the Little People, of the Welsh Castles and Fairy Rings and Haunted Houses. I really think Angela did believe in fairies and ghosts and Little People, for she said so wistfully one day – "I would dearly love to see a fairy!"'

In Polperro, where they still use the old-fashioned term for girls, Angela is spoken of as 'the old lady who wrote maids' books'. Hedley Libby, a retired fisherman, talks of taking her on his boat, *Petunia*, for two-hour trips along the west coast to Fowey, generally in the company of younger women. When The Haven was full of visitors, Dolly Milward would stay at his brother's house.

There were continual guests, and, of course, children's parties. There was one particularly memorable occasion when a child swallowed a moth along with his festive tea.

'Impossible!' Angela repeated over and over again, very upset. 'Impossible!'

Teas were garnished with cream. 'Delicious teas with cream and fruit,' said Doreen Corbett, who was made to take all the sand out of her shoes before climbing the steps to the cottage. 'Angel cake for tea,' recalled another guest, 'and Miss Brazil said it must always be eaten with strawberry jam and cream.' It was a striking contrast to the more frugal fare at other meals.

Carol Samuels, who slept there, said there was a stuffed seagull suspended from her bedroom ceiling. The visitor who partook of the angel cake was astonished by 'an ordinary dresser' in the sitting-room, 'with some china on it and all the shelves . . . edged with pink frills. Miss Brazil told me that the pink frills were her sister's work.' Probably it was Amy's travel china on its protective padding, moved to Polperro when Ffynnonbedr was sold.

Angela's impact was never negligible, and although she was considered a foreigner, the residents of Polperro owe a perpetual debt to her. Due to Angelica's early teaching she was passionately aware of the need for conservation, an environmentalist ahead of her time, and when, in 1922, she learned that land belonging to the ancient manor of Killigarth was being sold, she bought a portion, described as being part of Warren Field, for £550. She wrote to Marie Stopes:

> I have just bought the cliffs and hillside between Polperro and Talland. I heard they were for sale, and I was so afraid a specula-

tive builder might get them that I thought I had better save them before they could be spoilt. It makes a reserve for seagulls and primroses.

Five years later she was able to purchase a further strip of land which adjoined it. This time she paid £83 15s. od. and together the two areas totalled thirty-eight acres. When she died she left them to the National Trust.

She did not confine her altruistic gestures to Cornwall. She bequeathed a half of her royalties to charity, and during her lifetime, in 1938, she presented a cottage at Corley Moor to the Coventry Y.W.C.A., together with some furniture. The inaugural weekend, reported in a Coventry paper, was pure Angela Brazil.

Some thirty members and friends of the club were present at the opening of the cottage on Saturday afternoon by Miss Angela Brazil, the fairy godmother in the story.

Five of the members spent the weekend in the cottage and, from all accounts, a jolly good weekend it was too! The weather, of course, was not exactly all that could be desired for a weekend in the country but, nevertheless, the girls enjoyed themselves and were able to do a little exploring of the countryside.

On Sunday a number of girls from the club went out to the cottage for tea.

I was rather anxious to know if the proverbial ghost turned up to give the party that extra cheer, but nothing like that happened. The only ghostly figure that appeared was a broom covered with a sheet, a practical joke played on some of the unsuspecting members by a few of the girls.

The patriotism Angela had felt with fervour in the First World War, and which had imparted its flavour to her work, scarcely seems to have touched her in the second. In 1937 she wrote ardently to Marie Stopes: 'I am sure the Empire will rally round our new sovereign, whose Coronation was a wonderful event, and a landmark in national history,' but in the seven books published between 1940 and 1946 she made only token mention of the national cataclysm. There were none of those stirring perorations or instantly recognizable German spies, merely an Austrian refugee in the school, a refugee fund, and a handful of middle-class evacuees who were no different from any of the girls in any of the books. Living in Coventry she was not unaffected. Most nights were spent under the stairs, but the Brazils refused flatly to leave the city. The Quadrant was surrounded by sandbags, and when the cathedral was razed to the ground during the blitz, the familiar trio (Walter in the middle, a sister on either arm) walked each Sunday to Holy Trinity instead – a fact that was noted with some irony by those sensitive to the subtle social distinctions between Coventry's symbolic spires.

The raids which destroyed the cathedral and so much of Coventry took place on two successive nights, 14 and 15 November 1940, and there was a third the following May. In November the Y.W.C.A. hostel in The Butts was burnt out, but all the residents emerged safely from the shelter under the main building, and walked round to headquarters in Hertford Place. Most of the roof had gone, and the windows were shattered, but it was possible to cook breakfast on the open fires in the lounge and dining-room. Among the first helpers to arrive were Amy and Angela. Dressed in thick coats and gloves they worked for hours, clearing the broken glass from the conservatory, and stopping only once, in true British style, for cups of tea. A press report said that Angela Brazil had been on duty all day at the headquarters, helping the girls who were in Coventry for war work to make their arrangements for going home. It was a kind of apotheosis.

In 1945 Angela went to Scotland for local colour, staying near Helensburgh where the Blackies lived, and meeting Mr Walter Blackie while she was there. In August 1946 they published *The School on the Loch*. She began to write a new book, but she was becoming a little absent-minded. One sunny afternoon a friend saw her sitting on the edge of the pavement in Hertford Street, which was still a main thoroughfare of the town. She went and spoke to her, making the usual trite remarks about the weather, and suggested that she might like a cup of tea. Angela agreed and was escorted back to the nearby Quadrant. The maid (there was only one nowadays) opened the door, and the friend quickly explained the situation and left, Angela having by then forgotten she was there.

On 11 March 1947 she had supper as usual with Walter and Amy. She ate well, Amy said afterwards, and was in a gay mood. They all enjoyed the meal. The following morning they discovered that she had died in the night. On hearing the news someone in the Blackie office suggested it wouldn't be long before they received the manuscript of *The School at the Pearly Gates*.

Envoy

Angela Brazil liked to tie up her endings, and although it is no longer her story, I think her readers would like me to do the same. Walter Brazil lived only another four months, and Florence Brazil, once denied entrance to The Quadrant, was invited there by Amy to look after her. Visitors thought she was the housekeeper. Apart from small personal bequests, Amy left everything to her. Perhaps it was a condition of her acceptance, for the will was made just a few months after Walter's death. Florence said the Brazils had always detested and resented her and she must have felt there was a measure of poetic justice in the financial comfort she enjoyed in her old age.

Amy died on 19 January 1951 and Florence, Carol and Gilbert were the only mourners at the funeral service. 'The Brazils wrote love letters to each other,' said Florence disparagingly as she cleared out Amy's desk. 'Stupid sentimental stuff!' With Amy's other accumulated letters and household receipts she put them onto the fire.

The house had deteriorated, and water ran down from a leak behind the drawing-room wall. The major items of furniture went to Christie's and Florence disposed of the rest. Faith took the incomplete manuscript of the last Angela Brazil school story, and in 1974 decided that it could be of no possible interest to anyone and threw it away.

Appendix A

THE FORTUNES OF PHILIPPA

Chapter IX A Hard Time

'I have not that alacrity of spirit
Nor cheer of mind that I was wont to have.'

Time seemed to pass very rapidly away, and I could scarcely realize it when I found I had been more than a year at The Hollies. I was now a tall girl of thirteen, with a considerable idea of the dignity of my age, and much resented anyone alluding to me as 'a child'. My aunt thought me greatly improved, and spoke in warm praise of Mrs Marshall's system of education; while as for me, my life at San Carlos seemed such a past tale that it was difficult to believe I had ever been the forlorn little stranger who had landed in England with so many doubts and fears only three years ago. You must not think, however, that I had entirely forgotten my home and the dear old friends of my childhood. I still sent warm messages to Juanita and Tasso and the other members of our household, though I could no longer speak their language; and I liked to hear accounts of them in my father's letters, while I believe on their part they all looked forward to seeing their little signorita one day in their midst again. It was perhaps only natural after all that my new life should in some measure erase the old one from my mind; it was what my father had desired, and if I were beginning to think that England was far more to me than the country I had left, he would be the first to rejoice over my altered views. So far from feeling any danger of my affection for him being weakened, he knew that my change of opinions only tightened the bond between us, since the older and wiser I grew, so much the more would I be able to appreciate him and enjoy his companionship when we should meet again.

I was now in the third form at school, as I had been moved up with

Blanche, Janet, and Cathy, and found myself the youngest in a class which had a reputation both for quick wits and hard work. Miss Percy was our teacher, and, though in many respects an excellent one, she was a woman of narrow sympathies and strict discipline; very different from kindly Miss Buller, who had always tried to make the rough paths of learning as smooth as possible for our stumbling feet. Another disagreeable point of my promotion was that I had Ernestine Salt for a class-mate, and however much I might dislike her I must perforce be thrown continually into her society. As you may imagine, she did not welcome my advent, giving me to understand that she considered me an intruder among girls who were all older than myself, and that my advancement was only due to Mrs Marshall's partiality. Lucy had remained behind in the upper fourth. Never a very clever girl, she had little ambition, and was quite content if she could scrape along without incurring any specially severe reproof from her teachers. Though I loved her as my cousin, I felt she occupied quite a different place in my heart from my darling Cathy. It is perhaps only possible to have one very dearest friend, and while Cathy seemed to win all my love and admiration, and to appeal to everything that was highest and best in me, Lucy's tastes were based so much on the lines of Aunt Agatha that I found we had little in common. I saw less of her now than ever, for, Mary having come to The Hollies this term, Mrs Marshall had arranged for the sisters to sleep together, while to my great delight I was allowed to share a vacant bedroom with Cathy. We moved our household goods into our new quarters with much noise and chattering. My case of South American butterflies was accorded the place of honour over the chimney-piece, together with the portrait of my father; the brush which Cathy had won at the Everton Meet hung proudly over her wash-stand; my views of San Carlos were distributed about the walls; while photos of Marshlands and the Winstanley family in every conceivable position adorned our chests-of-drawers and dressing-table.

'I feel as if we were relations now you have come to share my room,' said Cathy. 'I've always longed for a younger sister, so I'm going to adopt you, Philippa dear, and try to believe that you're really and truly mine. You haven't any mother of your own, so I shall put *my* mother's photo in the middle of the dressing-table that she may belong to us both. She has always called you her second little daughter.'

I found the work in my new class taxed my exertions to the uttermost. Mrs Marshall had a very high standard as to what should be required from girls of our age, and it was only with the greatest difficulty I was able to keep up to it. Without Cathy's help I must most certainly have failed. She was a true friend in need. She would patiently go over my preparation with me, explaining difficult rules, repeating dates and vocabularies again and again to fix them in my memory, or showing me so clearly and concisely the reasons for the various problems in mathematics, that I felt I could learn more easily from her than from our teachers. My one haunting fear was that Mrs Marshall should consider me below the level of the class and should send me down again into the fourth, for to be thus banished from Cathy seemed the worst that fate could hold in store for me. Never very robust I worked far beyond my strength, and the continual strain began at last to tell upon my health. I grew thin and pale, I was troubled with a perpetual headache, and I sometimes indulged in unreasonable fits of crying, which incurred the severe reproof of Miss Percy, who had no sympathy with 'nerves'.

'I can't help it – I can't, indeed!' I confided to Cathy after one of these outbreaks. 'My head feels so chock full of facts I sometimes think it won't hold any more. When I look at my book the letters seem to dance before my eyes, and I mix up mathematics with history and want to talk German in the French class.'

'Tell Mrs Marshall, and ask her to knock something off,' suggested Cathy.

'No, no! She would only say the class was too difficult for me, and send me down, and unless I can stay up here with you and Janet life simply isn't worth living. Never mind, I'll manage to worry on somehow, if only Miss Percy would let me alone!'

Unfortunately that was exactly what Miss Percy would not do. She had taken it into her head that I was hysterical, and that my whims and fancies must not on any account be humoured. I dare say she thought she was only doing her duty, but she harried me continually. An untied hair-ribbon, a blot on my exercise, an ink-stain on my finger, or an awkward attitude in class, were occasions for instant and severe fault-finding. No doubt they were all little defects which called for amendment, but she made the mistake of dealing with them too hardly. I believe, if people would only realize it, that overwork and ill-health are often responsible for many tiresome habits in growing girls. It was certainly so in my case; I sat crooked because my back ached, I lolled on my desk because I was really tired, I fidgeted from sheer nervousness when I felt Miss Percy's eye upon me, and when, having brought down all the vials of her wrath upon my head, I ended by bursting into tears, it was hard to be accused of temper or sullenness when I felt I would have given the whole world for a kind word.

I think we all suffered much from the deadly sameness of our life. In the summertime we were allowed a considerable amount of leisure, which we spent in the garden at croquet, tennis, or archery, but during the winter months the play hours were greatly curtailed and extra classes added, while the only exercise we took was a short daily 'croco-dile' walk, with hockey for an hour on Wednesdays and Saturdays. Girls who are not boarders do not feel this lack of variety. The walk to and from school, and, above all, the different subjects which are discussed at home, make a change of thought and a wholesome break; but the monotony of spending week after week meeting no one except teachers and companions, discussing nothing but school topics, never seeing a newspaper or a magazine or hearing what is going on in the outside world, is apt to have a rather depressing influence upon some dispositions. The teachers, seeing us all day long, were inclined to worry too much over our small faults, while we on our side, having little else to distract our minds, were wont to magnify our woes out of all just proportion. Miss Percy's nagging only seemed to make my faults the worse.

'I never seem able to please her,' I grumbled one day at breakfast-time. 'If I say my lessons correctly she tells me I'm twitching my hands or wrinkling my forehead; and then if I try to think about my hands and my forehead the lessons go right out of my mind, so I'm wrong either way. It seems no use trying.'

'She's horribly mean,' sighed Janet, who suffered at times herself. 'My exercise was quite right yesterday, but she made me copy it all out again, just because I had four mistakes in spelling. It was really too bad.'

'I could forgive her the exercises,' said Millicent, 'if she'd only make stronger coffee. This cup of mine is simply dish-water. I wish Mrs Marshall would come down again at breakfast-time, it used to be ever so much better when she poured out.'

'Let us get up a round robin and beg her to come!' laughed Cathy. 'We could say we'd missed her charming conversation.'

'Quietly! Quietly!' said Miss Percy from the other end of the table, for Cathy had raised her voice above the low undertone in which we had been speaking.

'We might ask her to give "coffee" as the next conversation topic,' said Janet, 'and then Millicent could announce that she liked it strong, as her intelligent remark.'

'It's the chicory I object to,' said Millicent; 'I loathe the smell of it. I'm sure it oughtn't to have any in. Ought it, Phil?'

'Certainly not,' I replied. 'I wish you could have tasted the coffee we used to have at San Carlos. You'd never forget it. It came from our own plantations, and Pedro used to roast it and grind it just before he poured the water on. I've often watched him make it. That was really worth calling coffee.'

'Pity we can't import him over here to give the cook a lesson,' said Janet. 'But I expect there's something in the quality, and how much you put in the pot. Will you have another cup, Milly?'

'No, thank you! One is enough of this brew. Here comes the bread-and-butter plate. I hope it'll all be finished before it comes to me, for I don't want any more.'

Among many rules at The Hollies there was a law that nothing must be left upon the table, and the bread-and-butter was always severely passed round till the plate was empty. On this particular day I was not hungry, and when the last piece was offered to me I promptly declined it. Cathy quickly and quietly handed it on to Janet, who was in the very act of taking it when Miss Percy's voice bade her pause.

'Did I notice you refuse that piece of bread-and-butter, Philippa Seaton?' she asked.

'Yes, Miss Percy,' I replied.

'And why?'

'I'm not hungry,' I said nervously.

'But you know the rule?'

'I suppose I do.'

'Then why did you not take it?'

'I've had enough, Miss Percy,' I blurted out. 'I simply can't eat any more!'

She looked at me with infinite scorn.

'Cannot eat any more! Then you *must* have been greedy if you find it absolutely impossible to finish even this little piece. I will not urge you after such a plea, but I think you may well be ashamed of your excuse.'

I felt keenly the injustice of the suggestion, but I was powerless to retort. It was but a sample of her methods of training us, and to have 'answered back' would have been an offence liable to be visited with heavy punishment. So far from over-eating myself I had generally little appetite for breakfast, and made the merest apology for a meal. As a result of this, by eleven-o'clock recreation I would find I was wildly hungry, but as we had no lunch at The Hollies I was obliged to wait until the one-o'clock dinner, by which time I was almost faint for want of food. How often have I evaded Miss Percy's sharp eye, and, dodging down the back-staircase, have begged a piece of bread or a hot potato from the sympathetic cook, to be eaten surreptitiously behind my pocket-handkerchief in the playground! I have even bribed the house-maid to buy me biscuits and smuggle them into my locker, incurring thereby both the risk of her dismissal and my own disgrace, for it was one of the strictest rules of the school that the girls should obtain no private supplies.

It is, I suppose, almost impossible for any mistress, however cons-cientious, to give to forty different pupils the same care and attention as they would receive at home. I am sure Mrs Marshall thought she took every precaution to secure our health, and if I had been definitely ill or in pain she would have been kindness itself; but it is so difficult some-times to tell whether a girl is really ailing or only shirking her work, that unless we complained of special symptoms no notice was taken of our general condition, so my pale cheeks and increased lassitude passed without comment. I felt the meaning of the old adage: 'A sound mind in a sound body.' I found myself worrying most absurdly over trifles which would not have distressed me to nearly such an extent if I had been able to distract my thoughts. After all, school is one's little world, and a bad mark, an unjust reproof, or a quarrel with a companion at the time, seem as overwhelming troubles as any we may encounter in after-life.

Matters went on from bad to worse. In my struggles to keep up to the standard of my class I began the foolish habit of smuggling my books into my bedroom, that I might take a last glance at my lessons before I got into bed, and I would lie repeating French verbs or German grammatical rules to myself long after the gas in the passage had been turned out. It was but a natural consequence that I could not sleep. Night after night I have tossed and turned, trying first one side of my pillow and then the other to cool my burning head, counting the strokes as the clock struck midnight, and feeling as if the dead silence of the house grew almost unbearable. There is perhaps nothing so lonely as to lie awake while others sleep; the darkness of the room oppressed me, it was terrible to open my eyes and see nothing but blackness around me, out of which my imagination would conjure up ghostly figures stealing around my bed. Had I dared I would have begged for a night-light, but I knew full well that such fancies would meet with scant sympathy at Miss Percy's ears. The sound of Cathy's quiet breathing made me feel as though she were miles away, but I was not selfish enough to wake her up to console me in my misery, and after tossing about for hours I would at last fall asleep, to find the unwelcome bell ringing in my ears before I seemed out of my first troubled dream.

I woke up one morning, after a restless night such as this, feeling limp and irritable, and very unable to cope with the world in general. There was a tiresome rule at The Hollies that before we left our rooms we must take each sheet and blanket separately off our beds, fold them, and place them in a neat pile upon a chair.

'It's a stupid custom,' said Cathy, grumbling for the hundredth time as she struggled to get the four corners of her coverlet even. 'I can't imagine why we shouldn't turn the clothes over the end of the bed as we do at home. They would air just as well, or better. There's the bell ringing now, and I haven't my collar on! Be quick, Phil, let me help you to tie your hair. We must simply fly or we shall both be late.'

I had absolutely no time to arrange my bed. I seized the sheets and blankets all together, and, rolling them in one untidy bundle, I flung them upon a chair. I did not even look to see if the room were in order, but, buttoning my dress as I went, I tore down the passage, just in time to slip into the dining-room behind Cathy, as Mrs Marshall opened the Bible to read prayers. We began lessons immediately after breakfast. The whole school assembled first in the large class-room for call-over, and I had taken my place and was arranging my books in order, giving a last desperate glance at the dates in my history and the troublesome genealogy of the House of Stuart. We rose and curtsied when Miss Percy entered, and she bowed and wished us good-morning, in accordance with the formal etiquette which we practised at The Hollies, but instead of seating herself as usual, she placed a few things which I could not see upon the chair, and advanced a little forward with an air of more than usual gravity upon her face.

'Philippa Seaton,' she said impressively, 'I feel that I have borne long enough with your careless and shiftless ways. For some time now I have made every effort to help you to cure yourself of many bad habits, but instead of seeing any improvement it appears to me that you allow yourself to neglect even the ordinary rules of the school. This morning I visited your bedroom. I found your bed-clothes in utter confusion upon a chair, your nail-brush evidently unused, your comb left full of hairs upon the dressing-table, a pair of boots, a slipper, and a shoehorn lying upon the floor, while this bag full of cotton reels was flung under your wash-stand. I am determined that for once I will teach you a lesson, and I shall pin these articles on to your back, in the hope that by showing your disgrace to the whole school I may help you to remember to be more neat and orderly in the future. Come here!'

In much fear and trembling I approached her. She turned to the chair, where (it would have been ludicrous if it had not all been so horribly solemn) my comb, my boots, my slipper, my shoe-horn, and my bag of cottons lay piled in a tragic little heap. She fastened them securely on to my dress with safety-pins, till I looked like a gipsy pedlar or an old clotheswoman, and bade me return to my place. Burning with indignation I sat down. All my pride was wounded and the tears came swimming into my eyes. I felt she had no right to treat me thus. There were certain fair and recognized penalties for neglected duties at which I should not have rebelled, but to be made a laughing-stock for the whole school was out of all proportion to my offence. I could see the amused smile with which Ernestine Salt nudged her companion, and knew how unmercifully she would tease me afterwards, and the thought that I must spend the entire morning with these absurd things dangling on my back was almost more than my spirit could brook. I gulped back my tears sufficiently to answer 'present' when my name was called, and sat, fighting with my face and trying not to feel that every girl in the room was looking at me. There was a slight tug at my dress behind, and Cathy cautiously thrust a tiny scrap of paper into my hand. I managed to read it unobserved: 'She's the hatefullest thing that ever was,' it ran. 'But never mind; don't let her think you care.' I scrunched up the paper and held up my head. After all, why should I care? I had committed no very desperate sin, and I knew that nearly everyone must be secretly in sympathy with me. I would brave it out, and show Miss Percy that though she might inflict any punishment she chose she was not able to crush my spirit entirely. As to Ernestine Salt, I would defy her, sneer as she might. It was unfortunate for me that my first lesson of the day should be with Miss Percy. With the wretched boots and bobbins sticking into me whenever I attempted to lean back in my seat, I felt in anything but a docile or tractable frame of mind, and, though she certainly would not have allowed it, I do not think she herself was in the best of tempers. She corrected Janet sharply for stooping, reduced Millicent to the very verge of tears, and even found fault with Cathy's beautifully neat and tidy exercise. We were learning the geography of India, a large map of which hung over the black-board, and in the course of the lesson we were each required in turn to indicate the positions of certain rivers and cities of the Punjaub. I was sitting in class next to Ernestine Salt, and as I rose hastily up to step forward and take the pointer, she suddenly put out her foot, as if by chance, exactly at the moment when I passed her. I tripped, made a desperate effort to save myself, caught wildly at the easel, and fell, sending black-board, map, pegs, pointer, and all with a horrible crash on to the floor.

There was dead silence in the room as I picked myself up. Miss Percy raised the fallen easel and the torn map, and looked at me with white lips.

'What is the meaning of this, Philippa Seaton?' she asked.

'I couldn't help it,' I answered, rather sullenly I am afraid. 'I – I believe I tripped.'

'No other girl has tripped. You are either irredeemably awkward or have caused this accident by deliberate intention. I very much fear it is the latter.'

'You've no right to say so!' I burst out defiantly, roused out of all discipline by her tone. 'I've told you I couldn't help it, and if you can't believe my word I should like you to take me to Mrs Marshall.'

'You shall certainly go to Mrs Marshall when she is at liberty,' replied Miss Percy in freezing tones. 'But in the meantime I am not going to interrupt the lesson on your behalf. You will stand there by the door, holding the broken pointer in your hand, till the class is over.'

I do not think Miss Percy was altogether happy at that moment, but I am sure she was not so miserable as I. I knew well I had done wrong to answer her so rudely, and the sense of my own shortcomings, added to the feeling of hot wrath against her injustice and unkindness, made it the most horribly difficult thing in the world to stand there, the target for all eyes. My head ached as if it would burst, and I rested my weary weight first on one foot and then on another. Each minute felt hours to me as the lesson slowly dragged along. I pressed my trembling hands together, and tried with a desperate effort to keep my eyes steadily fixed on the clock over the chimney-piece; but somehow the figures all seemed at once to be mixed together, the room swam before me in a kind of blur, I heard Miss Percy's voice as if it were a very long way off asking me something I could not hear, and then all was utter darkness.

When I came to myself I was lying on the sofa in the library. Mrs Marshall was bending over me, bathing my head with eau de Cologne, and Miss Buller was fanning me with a palm-leaf screen.

'Are you better, my dear?' asked Mrs Marshall anxiously. 'Don't try to get up. Drink this glass of water and lie down again.'

'What happened?' I asked. 'How did I come here?'

'You fainted in the class-room, but you must not talk about it now. I wish you to rest for a while, and then Miss Buller shall bring you some beef-tea.'

'I don't want any, thank you!' I said, trying to raise myself a little, but my head swam so strangely and I felt so giddy and queer that I was glad to sink back again upon the sofa cushions.

'I think we had better put you to bed,' said Mrs Marshall, adding in an undertone to Miss Buller: 'If she is not better by this evening, I shall certainly send for the doctor.'

I was not better by the evening; my hands were burning hot, and my head felt so unusually light that I could scarcely recognize the many people who seemed to come in and out of my room. I knew that when I asked for water Miss Buller was always ready with the glass in her hand, I thought once that Cathy was sobbing quietly behind the curtain of my bed, and I am certain that Mrs Marshall never left me all night.

'It is a decided case of nervous breakdown, due to overwork,' I heard the doctor saying. 'You must keep her very quiet, and I will see her again in the morning.'

There were no more lessons for me that term. As soon as I was well enough to travel Aunt Agatha took me herself for a fortnight to Brighton, where the restful uneventful days and the invigorating sea-breezes soon brought back the roses to my cheeks, and gave me untroubled sleep and peaceful dreams at night. I think this episode, and something which the doctor had said, must have caused Mrs Marshall seriously to reconsider the rules of the school and the hours of our work. She was a sensible woman, most conscientious over our well-being, and ever ready to adopt new ideas if she believed them to be better than the old ones. When I returned to school at the beginning of the next term, I found that our time-table was completely changed. The hours of work were considerably relaxed, and instead of the stupid walks up and down the high-road, we were taken almost daily rambles over the hills or in the beautiful woods by the river. Miss Percy had mysteriously disappeared, and her place was filled by a new teacher who was fond of natural history, and who encouraged us to find specimens of stones, leaves, or flowers, explaining them with so much enthusiasm that the stupidest girl could not fail to be interested. The new scheme answered well; the extra time given to outdoor recreation was not wasted, for we went back to our books with fresh zeal; and I think we really got through as much work as we had done before, if not in the actual number of pages learnt, at any rate in the amount we remembered afterwards.

Appendix B

Local poet Abe Jephcott's tribute to the Brazils after he had visited The Quadrant in October 1939 when Angela was seventy.

CONNOISSEURS

At the head of the grand staircase
She received me.
Angela . . .
Ah! She stood as a statue would
New found in the Isles of Greece,
Enrobed in gold and jewelled fold
Of emerald green and bright cerise.

'Twas sunlight at meridian height,
Slanting through the window panes
Of old stained glasswork in the background
Armour bright with spears and chains.

I saw a wild rose touch her cheek . . .
Then winter took a stand
As drooping clouds obscured the sky
To make wonder light upon her hand.

As it rested on the balustrade
And the classic contour of her face
All the seasons seemed so near,
And all the gods were saying grace.

Upon it we exchanged a look!
The world flew open as a book
At the page of life where mortals meet
And pass the frontiers to the soul.

Life and art, art and life . . .

We talked of pods and the sycamore tree
Roof tops and vista of old Coventree,
Away o'er the Green to three precious spires,
'Sermons in stone' to match high desires.

For a tour of the house, enchantment was laid
By the inlay of pearl, the porcelain, the jade,
Riches in pictures and caskets antique,
Old dressers in oak and craftwork in teak.

I felt my heart beat at seeing these things.
And the atmosphere drawn from amethyst rings
Made floats on the air so easy to see
In inmost thoughts of the lady and me.

But in the great salon we loitered,
We were kneeling on the floor,
When the King of Connoisseurs entered
Through the heavy panelled door.

He was old and tall and silver white,
Sweet thawed into an old world grace,
The love of art shone in his eyes
And etched fine lines on his classic face.

He showed me a spinet
On which Pepys had played,
Then old fashioned furniture deftly inlaid
By workers in tulip and rare ivory,
Finger tipped roses in ace marquetry.

And how the quaint pieces in pewter and oak
Looked soberly grand as timepieces spoke,
In the deep song of England my own,
And the sweet bells of France all of a tone,
Till time seemed all heaven planned
And strangely alone –
To me in my trance and she in her own.

Ah! No trance; she stood so near
Beneath the crystal chandelier,
Angela . . .
Clear cut as the diamond glass above
Queen of literature and art's own love.

*

On the stone flagged ancient floor
Near the iron bound portal door
We heard the bell sing Au Revoir! . . .

151

Dream ye of pods and the sycamore tree,
The roof tops and spires of old Coventree,
Art within art is a passion in thee,
Blue eyes and brown eyes in connoisseurs three.

Bibliography

The Mischievous Brownie, T. W. Patterson, Edinburgh, 1899.
Contributions to *Our School Magazine*, T. W. Patterson, Edinburgh, 1900.
The Fairy Gifts, T. W. Patterson, Edinburgh, 1901.
Contributions to *Our School Magazine*, T. W. Patterson, Edinburgh, 1901.
Contributions to *Burgon's Magazine*, Atlantic Press Ltd, Manchester, 1902.
Contributions to *Our School Magazine*, T. W. Patterson, Edinburgh, 1902.
The Enchanted Fiddle, T. W. Patterson, Edinburgh, 1903.
'Twixt Love and Duty', *Burgon's Magazine*, Atlantic Press Ltd, Manchester, 1903.
Contribution to *Our School Magazine*, T. W. Patterson, Edinburgh, 1903.
Four Recitations, T. W. Patterson, Edinburgh, 1903.
Contributions to *Burgon's Magazine*, Atlantic Press Ltd, Manchester, 1903.
Fairy tales, etc., *Our School Magazine*, T. W. Patterson, Edinburgh, 1904.
The Wishing Princess, T. W. Patterson, Edinburgh, 1904.
Contribution to *Burgon's Magazine*, Atlantic Press Ltd, Manchester, 1904.
'A Winter in Palestine' (account of personal visit), *Burgon's Magazine*, Atlantic Press Ltd, Manchester, 1905.
A Terrible Tomboy (illustrated by Amy and Angela Brazil), Gay & Bird, 1904; Oxford, 1914 (2nd ed.); Readers' Juvenile Library, 1932 (sixpenny ed.).
The Fortunes of Philippa, Blackie & Son, 1906.
The Third Class at Miss Kay's, Blackie & Son, 1908.
The Nicest Girl in the School, Blackie & Son, 1909.

'The Guinea Pig's Visit', *Little Folks*, Cassell & Co., 1909.
'The Feast in No. 7', *Little Folks*, Cassell & Co., 1909.
Bosom Friends, Nelson & Co., 1909.
Our School Record, Dow & Lester, 1909.
The Manor House School, Blackie & Son, 1910.
'The New Girl at Miss Gordon's', *Little Folks*, Cassell & Co., 1910.
'A Moorland Sketch', *Girls' Realm*, Cassell & Co., 1910.
'Who Stole the Toffee?' *Little Folks*, Cassell & Co., 1910.
'Ruth's Penny Squirt', *Little Folks*, Cassell & Co., 1910.
'The Rebellion of Betty', *Little Folks*, Cassell & Co., 1910.
'A Picture Postcard', *Girls' Realm*, Cassell & Co., 1910.
'Monitress Mary', *Red Book for Girls*, Oxford, 1910.
'What Happened on the Ici', *Little Folks*, Cassell & Co., 1911.
'Jill's Red Pinafore', *Little Folks*, Cassell & Co., 1911.
'Will o' the Wisp', *British Girls' Annual*, Cassell & Co., 1911.
'Miss Trelawny B.A.', *British Girls' Annual*, Cassell & Co., 1911.
'The Old Inn at Bellasa', *Girls' Realm*, Cassell & Co., 1911.
'An Aversion in Grey', *Girls' Realm*, Cassell & Co., 1911.
The New Girl at St Chad's, Blackie & Son, 1911.
A Fourth Form Friendship, Blackie & Son, 1911.
'A Schoolgirl's Dilemma', *Green Book for Girls*, Oxford, 1911.
A Pair of Schoolgirls, Blackie & Son, 1912.
'While Father was Away', *Little Folks*, Cassell & Co., 1912.
'A Runaway Picnic', *Little Folks*, Cassell & Co., 1912.
'Margaret's Room-mate', *British Girls' Annual*, Cassell & Co., 1912.
'The Tactics of Decima', *British Girls' Annual*, Cassell & Co., 1913.
'A Hard Term', *British Girls' Annual*, Cassell & Co., 1913.
'A School Hostage', *Blue Book for Girls*, Oxford, 1913.
The Youngest Girl in the Fifth, Blackie & Son, 1913.
The Leader of the Lower School, Blackie & Son, 1913.
The School by the Sea, Blackie & Son, 1914.
The Girls of St Cyprians, Blackie & Son, 1914.
'The Chetwold Scholarship', *Violet Book for Girls*, Oxford, 1914.
'The Prefect of the Third Form', *Violet Book for Girls*, Oxford, 1914.
'An Entrance Examination', *British Girls' Annual*, Cassell & Co., 1914.
'A Midnight Revel', *British Girls' Annual*, Cassell & Co., 1914.
'All in a Fog', *Girls' Realm*, Cassell & Co., 1914.
For the Sake of the School, Blackie & Son, 1915.
The Jolliest Term on Record, Blackie & Son, 1915.
'How Kathsie Scored', *Rose Book for Girls*, Oxford, 1915.
'The Event of the Term', *British Girls' Annual*, Cassell & Co., 1915.
'A Stolen Bonfire', *Little Folks*, Cassell & Co., 1915.
'The Brownies', *Blackie's Annual*, Blackie & Son, 1915.
The Luckiest Girl in the School, Blackie & Son, 1916.
'While Frank had Measles', *The Jolly Book*, T. Nelson & Son, 1916.
'The Refugees', *The Jolly Book*, T. Nelson & Son, 1916.

BIBLIOGRAPHY

'Mixed Pickles', *The Jolly Book*, T. Nelson & Son, 1916.
'Freda's Foundling', *Little Folks*, Cassell & Co., 1916.
'The Turton Tennis Cup', *British Girls' Annual*, Cassell & Co., 1916.
'The Very Limit', *Blackie's Annual*, Blackie & Son, 1916.
The Madcap of the School, Blackie & Son, 1917.
'Back to the Land', *Blackie's Annual*, Blackie & Son, 1917.
The Slap Bang Boys, T. Nelson & Son, 1917.
'St Hilda's Hostel', *British Girls' Annual*, Cassell & Co., 1917.
'A Kindergarten Kid', *Little Folks*, Cassell & Co., 1918.
'The Third Form Strike', *British Girls' Annual*, Cassell & Co., 1918.
'The Butterfly Hunters', *Children's Annual*, Cassell & Co., 1918.
'Queen of the Dormitory', *British Girls' Annual*, Cassell & Co., 1918.
A Patriotic Schoolgirl, Blackie & Son, 1918.
For the School Colours, Blackie & Son, 1918.
'The Khaki Boys', *The Jolly Book*, T. Nelson & Son, 1918.*
'A Gift From the Sea', *The Chummy Book*, T. Nelson & Son, 1918.*
'Straight & Curley', 1919.*
'The Scallywag Boys', *The Jolly Book*, T. Nelson & Son, 1919.*
'The Treasure of the Woods', Oxford, 1919.
'The Language of Flowers', Oxford, 1919.
'The Cardiff Express', *Little Folks*, Cassell & Co., 1919.
'A Half Term Holiday', *British Girls' Annual*, Cassell & Co., 1919.
The Head Girl at The Gables, Blackie & Son, 1919.
A Harum Scarum Schoolgirl, Blackie & Son, 1919.
'The Scratching Ghost', *British Girls' Annual*, Cassell & Co., 1919.
Two Little Scamps and a Puppy, T. Nelson & Son, 1919.
'The School Picnic' or 'Sylvia's Saturday Tea Party', *Mrs Strang'
Annual*, Oxford, 1919.
'The Tradition of the School', *Little Folks*, Cassell & Co., 1919.
Loyal to the School, Blackie & Son, 1920.
A Popular Schoolgirl, Blackie & Son, 1920.
The Princess of the School, Blackie & Son, 1920.
'Betty's Birthday Cake', *Blackie's Annual*, Blackie & Son, 1920.
A Fortunate Term, Blackie & Son, 1921.
Loyal to the School, Blackie & Son, 1921.
The School in the South, Blackie & Son, 1922.
Monitress Merle, Blackie & Son, 1922.
Little Women (article), *Xmas Bookman*, Blackie & Son, 1922.
Schoolgirl Kitty, Blackie & Son, 1923.
'The Fairy Ring', *Blackie's Girls' Annual*, Blackie & Son, 1923.
'The Luck of the School', *Blackie's Girls' Annual*, Blackie & Son, 1923.
'The West Wing at the Manor', *Graphic*, 1923.
Captain Peggie, Blackie & Son, 1924.
'Win's First Week at School', *Girls' Budget*, Blackie & Son, 1924.
'An Exciting Picnic', *Blackie's Girls' Annual*, Blackie & Son, 1924.

* These four stories were afterwards published together in book form.

'The Last Day of the Holidays', *Blackie's Children's Annual*, Blackie & Son, 1924.

My Own Schooldays, Blackie & Son, 1925.

'A Little Too Clever', *Girls' Budget*, Blackie & Son, 1925.

'Flowers & Folklore' (article), *Blackie's Girls' Annual*, Blackie & Son, 1925.

Joan's Best Chum, Blackie & Son, 1926.

Queen of the Dormitory and Other Stories, Cassell & Co., 1926.

'Cornish Pisky Folk' (article), *Blackie's Annual*, Blackie & Son, 1926.

Ruth of St Ronan's, Blackie & Son, 1927.

'The Craft of Story Telling' (article), *Blackie's Girls' Annual*, Blackie & Son, 1927.

'Lucky Customs & Superstitions' (article), *Blackie's Girls' Annual*, Blackie & Son, 1927.

At School with Rachel, Blackie & Son, 1928.

St Catherine's College, Blackie & Son, 1929.

'Children's Games & Their Origins' (article), *Blackie's Girls' Annual*, Blackie & Son, 1930.

The Little Green School, Blackie & Son, 1931.

'Popular Fairy Tales and Their Origins' (article), *Blackie's Girls' Annual*, Blackie & Son, 1931.

Nesta's New School, Blackie & Son, 1932.

Jean's Golden Term, Blackie & Son, 1934.

The School at The Turrets, Blackie & Son, 1935.

An Exciting Term, Blackie & Son, 1936.

Jill's Jolliest School, Blackie & Son, 1937.

The School on the Cliff, Blackie & Son, 1938.

'Good Luck' (article), *Girls' Own Paper*, Blackie & Son, 1938.

'An Emergency School', *Girls' Own Paper*, Blackie & Son, 1939.

The School on the Moor, Blackie & Son, 1939.

'The Queer Girl at St Quentin's', *Girls' Own Paper*, Blackie & Son, 1940.

The New School at Scawdale, Blackie & Son, 1940.

Five Jolly Schoolgirls, Blackie & Son, 1941.

'Hallo Twins', *Girls' Own Paper*, Blackie & Son, 1941.

The Mystery of the Moated Grange, Blackie & Son, 1942.

The Secret of the Border Castle, Blackie & Son, 1943.

The School in the Forest, Blackie & Son, 1944.

Three Terms at Uplands, Blackie & Son, 1945.

The School on the Loch, Blackie & Son, 1946.

Omnibus Books published in 1937, 1961 (two vols.).

Index